Soviet Union

Editor Dale Gunthorp
Design Peter Benoist
Picture Research Maggie Colbeck
Production Philip Hughes
Illustrations Ron Hayward Associates
John Shackell
Marilyn Day
John Mousdale
Tony Payne
Maps Matthews and Taylor Associates
Consultants Bryan Woodriff, Senior
Lecturer in Liberal Studies, Kingston
Polytechnic; Stephen le Fleming, Lecturer
in Russian, University of Durham,
Svetlana le Fleming

Photographic sources Key to position of
illustrations: *(T)* top, *(C)* centre, *(B)*
bottom, *(L)* left, *(R)* right.
Associated Press *13(TR)*. B.B.C.
Copyright Photographs *26(BC)*. Colin
Craig *28(BL)*, *47(C)*. Tony Duffy *18(BC)*,
19(TL), *19(TR)*, *34(T)*. Henry Grant
21(CL), *46(TL)*, *52(BL)*. Keystone Press
Agency *45(BR)*, *53(CR)*. Mansell
Collection *9(TR)*, *13(C)*, *37(BL)*,
40(TL), *40(BL)*, *42(TR)*. John Massey

Stewart *6*, *24(TC)*, *25(BR)*, *35(BR)*,
42(C). Dennis Moore *2*, *8(TC)*, *14(B)*,
16(TL), *16(B)*, *17(TL)*, *17(TR)*,
17(BL), *18(T)*, *19(BL)*, *20(C)*, *21(BR)*,
22(TL), *23(BR)*, *24(BC)*, *24(BL)*,
26(TL), *27(BC)*, *28(TC)*, *29(TR)*,
29(BL), *30(T)*, *31(TR)*, *31(BL)*, *32(B)*,
33(TL), *39(BR)*, *40(BC)*, *43(BL)*,
46(BL), *49(C)*, *51(TR)*, *51(B)*, *52(T)*.
Novosti *9(BR)*, *14(C)*, *19(BR)*, *23(BL)*,
37(BR), *38(C)*, *48(B)*, *49(T)*, *49(CR)*,
52(T), *53(C)*. Potshots *53(CL)*. Radio
Times Hulton Picture Library *44(C)*.
Recontre *12(BR)*, *23(TL)*, *23(TR)*,
27(TR), *29(BR)*, *33(C)*, *36(T)*, *39(C)*,
44(T), *45(BL)*, *46(BR)*. Servizio
Editoriale Fotografico *13(TL)*, *26(BL)*,
33(BR), *35(TL)*, *35(BL)*, *37(TR)*,
37(B), *42(B)*, *43(TR)*. Society for
Cultural Relations with the U.S.S.R.
13(BL), *37(TL)*, *41(BR)*. Bryan
Woodriff *8(TL)*, *13(BR)*, *17(BR)*,
24(TL), *27(TL)*, *33(TR)*, *34(B)*,
38(BC), *38(TL)*, *43(TL)*, *51(TC)*.
The Trade Development Bank kindly
assisted by providing notes for the
photograph of currency.

First published 1975
Macdonald Educational Limited
Holywell House
London, E. C. 2

© Macdonald Educational
Limited 1975

ISBN 0 356 05099 8

Published in the United
States by Silver Burdett
Company, Morristown, N. J.
1976 Printing

Library of Congress
Catalog Card No. 75-44865

The endpaper picture shows the spires
of Cathedrals in the Kremlin.

Page 6, A May Day parade in Red Square.

Soviet Union

the land and its people

George Morey

Macdonald Educational

Contents

Invaders and settlers

The beginnings of Rus

The ancient Greeks knew southern Russia. They thought the valley of the Dnieper a wonderful region, producing quantities of fish, cattle and grain. It was a region which tempted invaders. The Eastern Slavs were most important among these; they moved westwards behind the great migrations of the Goths and Huns.

At an early date Norsemen from the Baltic came south into Russia in search of trade and adventure. The Slavs later joined the Norsemen in their ventures, and the year 862 A.D., when Rurik, the Norseman, is said to have captured Novgorod, is an important date in Russian history.

The Slav lands later became known as Rus, and the principal city, Kiev, grew rich. Under Prince Vladimir (980–1015 A.D.), Kiev Rus became Christian. The greatness of Kiev Rus lasted for little more than 300 years. Enemies closed in. In 1223, the Mongols invaded for the first time, causing great destruction, in their quest for money and slaves.

The growth of Moscow

At this time, Moscow was unimportant. It is not even mentioned until 1147! But it grew as Kiev and other rivals declined. It was a refuge for people fleeing from the Mongols; it bought protection by collecting tribute for the invaders; it lay on important trade routes, and it had a number of able princes.

By the time of Ivan the Great, the future shape of Russian history had become clear. Moscow had become an important State, dominating its neighbours. The Church, closely linked with the Greek Church, had become great and wealthy, and its influence was to last for a thousand years. Finally, whatever its rulers wanted to do, the strength of its western and northern neighbours forced Moscow to look eastwards. In later years, Moscow pushed its Empire east to the Pacific Ocean. It was not until the eighteenth century that Russia began to play an important role in the affairs of the West. At home, after 1922, Russia became stronger still, as leader in the Soviet Union.

▲ *The Bogatyars* (warriors), a painting by Vasnetsov (1898). This picture shows three folk-heroes of early Russian history, when Kiev Rus was the centre of Russian civilization and Vladimir I ruled. They are mounted on Steppe ponies.

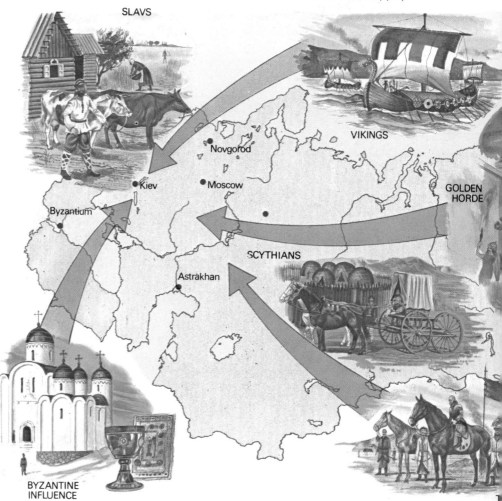

8

The gleaming spires of St. Sophia's Cathedral Kiev. Although the Russian church owed much to St. Cyril and the Greek Orthodox Church, it developed a beautiful style of architecture of its own.

Invaders of different eras settle the land

◄ The lands now forming the Soviet Union have been settled by many different peoples. Slavs, Norsemen and Sythians were among the early arrivals. The civilization of Byzantium spread from the south, and gradually all the cultures merged.

▼ Ivan IV, the Terrible (1533–84). He was the first Russian ruler to call himself Czar. He was a successful military leader and had sound ideas about the need to develop trade with the West. But he was brutally cruel.

▲ Novgorod as it appeared in the Middle Ages. This ancient city was then a flourishing republic and centre of trade.

Many lands in one state

Biggest country on earth

The Soviet Union is a vast country. It covers a sixth of the earth's land-area. It is more than twice as big as either the United States or China. It is approximately 5,000 kilometres from north to south, and over 9,500 kilometres from east to west.

Its population, however, is less than a third as large as that of China. To make matters more complex, large areas of the Soviet Union have few or no people. While most of the land lies in Asia, about two-thirds of the population lives in the European area. There are great extremes of climate. The northern part lies within the Arctic Circle, and there are areas where only mosses and lichens grow. Much of the Soviet Union has cold winters, but the coldest region is Siberia. Verkhoyansk is said once to have recorded a temperature of $-70°C$ $(-94°F)$! Even more important is the great range of temperature. Verkhoyansk has had a summer temperature of $36.7°C$ $(98°F)$. In the far south, however, there are areas where tea and cotton grow, and desert areas where the camel is used for transport. One interesting area is the Steppes, which stretch in a wide band eastwards from the Ukraine. This vast, almost treeless, area has very fertile soil, and produces excellent crops.

The variety of peoples

Other places which are well known to visitors and to Soviet citizens are the holiday resorts in the Crimea and around the Black Sea. They have a warm climate for a large part of the year.

So large a country is naturally the home of many peoples, of whom the Russians are the biggest and most influential group. The languages and customs of some peoples seem very strange even to Russians, although it is planned that everybody in the Soviet Union will one day be able to speak fluent Russian. (The different nationalities are looked at more closely on pages 46 and 47.) Though the Soviet Union is one country, its lands and peoples are among the most diverse of any nation on Earth.

Leningrad. A portrait of Peter the Great who built the city; a poster showing the cruiser "Aurora" which fired the first shot in the November revolution.

▲ **Moscow.** The Bell Tower of Ivan the Terrible; an icon; a dancer of the Bolshoi Ballet; and Moscow's underground.

▼ **The Ukraine.** St. Sophia's Cathedral, Kiev, and wheat fields. There was fierce fighting here between 1941 and 1945.

▲ **Odessa.** The Odessa Steps, made famous in the film *The Battleship Potemkin*; the Black Sea coast; and Joseph Stalin.

◄ The icebreaker *Lenin* was the first nuclear ship, with her is the world's largest diesel icebreaker.

▲ There is much heavy industry today in the Urals around Sverdlovsk and Magnitogorsk.

▲ Siberia has been a place of exile ever since the days of the Czars.

▲ The flying-ambulance, a YAK-12, can reach the most inaccessible spots in Siberia. Gold is mined and bears are hunted in Siberia.

▲ The Russian whaling fleets from the ports on the Pacific Ocean make regular trips to the Antarctic. A train on the Great Trans-Siberian railway passes the small rural station of Smolyaninivo.

▼ Soviet soldiers on the Chinese border.

▼ The Space Centre at Baikonur. Cotton-picking near Tashkent and the city of Bukhara in Uzbekistan.

▲ The great hydro-electric station at Bratsk in Siberia. Below, a nomadic tribe with their tents made of skins, and a Mongol horseman from Central Asia.

Arctic Circle
Verkhoyansk
Verkhoyansk Mountains
Arctic Circle
River Lena
River Ob
River Yenisei
Ural Mountains
Trans-Siberian railway
Yablonovyi Mountains
Lake Baikal
Omsk
Novosibirsk
Irkutsk
original route
Vladivostok
Baikonur
Lake Balkhash
Mongolia
Alma Ata

Russia
China

12·4·61

11

Soviet influence on the world

Growth of a great power

By the 1920s, Russia had ceased to be a great power. She had been defeated in war by Germany, and was torn by civil war and revolution. In little over fifty years, the Soviet Union has become one of the two greatest powers in the world. This has been achieved by hard work and sacrifices.

At the end of the Second World War in 1945, the dogged resistance of the Russian peoples to their invaders won many admirers in the West. But this support did not long outlive the war. In peace old hostilities flared up again, and the growing Soviet military might was seen as a threat. Today, the Soviet army is very big and her defence expenditure is greater than that of the United States. The Soviet navy is to be found in every ocean, and recently, activity in the Mediterranean and the Indian Ocean has been increased. In 1962, the sending of giant Russian rockets to Cuba, a small Communist country, made war between the United States and the Soviet Union seem a real danger.

Small countries on Russia's western borders have felt her presence. The republics of Lithuania, Latvia and Estonia were overrun by Soviet troops during World War Two, and they are now part of the Soviet Union. Poland, East Germany, Hungary and Bulgaria all have Communist governments sympathetic to the Soviet Union.

Working for peace

The Soviet Union has taken an important part in the work of the United Nations ever since its foundation, and has matched the work of other powers in helping underdeveloped peoples. The Soviet Union has also spent much time and money in furthering its ideal of world peace.

Like every other nation, the Soviet Union has need of friends and supporters. A great deal of money is therefore spent all over the world in telling foreigners about the Soviet Union, in arranging visits and study courses. Among its best "ambassadors" are the teams of young men and women, who are taking an ever-growing part in international sport and cultural events. In a different sphere, the work of such musicians as David Oistrakh and Svyatoslav Richter, of composers such as Shostakovich, and the wonderful performances of the ballet companies, have found many admirers.

The international influence of Leninism

▲ From the beginning, the followers of Lenin have been conscious of the important part women play in society. In 1918, though much engaged with troubles in Russia, Lenin held discussions with Sylvia Pankhurst, the English political leader. She campaigned for women's rights and for the poor of British cities.

▲ Karl Marx called upon the workers of the world to unite. The Soviet Government has devoted much energy and spent millions of pounds in its efforts to spread Marx and Lenin's socialism over the world.

▲ A march of the Italian Communist party in 1945 demanding peace and employment. Lenin's international policy helped Communist parties in countries like Italy to become established.

▼ China, the country with the largest population in the world, adopted a form of socialism derived from the theories of Lenin in 1949. Although today China and the Soviet Union are not very friendly, Marx and Lenin are still admired.

▲ Ivan Petrovitch Pavlov (1849–1936), the Russian scientist, who studied the hidden reasons why creatures behave in certain ways. In the experiments, he rang a bell every time he fed a dog, until the dog became used to the idea. After that, the dog's mouth watered every time the bell rang.

▼ Laika, the dog, was the first creature sent into space. She was part of an experiment to see whether humans could survive similar flights. There was world-wide indignation that the Russians had no plans to bring Laika back to earth.

▲ A Soviet soldier raises the Red Flag above the Berlin Reichstag, 1945. It had taken the Soviet army six days of bitter fighting to force their way 30 miles to the heart of Germany. This was the moment of triumph in World War II.

◄ Tchaikovsky (1840–93), one of the greatest of Russian composers. His symphonies are often performed today, and it is difficult to understand why his work was often criticized when first performed. His work only became popular after his death.

▼ The construction of the Aswan Dam in Egypt. This dam controls the waters of the River Nile. It is one of the many overseas projects which the Soviet Union has supported with money and technical help. In return, the Soviet Union has gained friendship and trade contacts in countries like Egypt.

▲ Soviet tanks in Prague, 1968. Since the War, there has been rivalry between the world powers, each wanting more influence. The Soviet Union has great political and economic power in a semi-circle of states lying between itself and Western Europe. In 1968 the Soviet army invaded Czechoslovakia to suppress a movement for liberalized rule.

Home life

Dealing with the housing problem

After the Revolution thousands of country dwellers crowded into the cities, causing a terrible housing problem. Several families often had to share a single room!

The Soviet Government has tackled the problem seriously. Even so, in the big towns there are thousands of communal apartments where people have to share a kitchen and toilet.

More people, however, are now being housed in large blocks of flats. Most of the flats are small, and a family of four is not likely to get more than two rooms with a kitchen and bathroom. These families are none the less fortunate because rents, and the cost of gas and electricity, are kept low.

Even so, the life of many city dwellers seems hard. Both parents usually go out to work, and if there is no "babushka" (grandmother) to help, there is a great deal to do before setting out. The children usually make up the divans in the living-room where they sleep, and tidy the room. But the mother has a busy time, seeing that everything is in order, cooking the breakfast and getting a mid-morning snack ready. All too often, fathers give no help at all. School holidays, when the children are at home, present a problem and many women worry about their children during the day.

When work is over

For many people work finishes about five o'clock, and they hope to be home before six, unless they are attending meetings at their place of work. Most people will have had their lunch in the works' canteen, so that supper is a simple meal during the week.

Soviet people are great readers, and spend a lot of their leisure reading newspapers and novels. They may, if they prefer, watch television. T.V. sets are among the consumer goods—like new furniture and refrigerators—which have become more freely available. There are cinemas and concerts, and, if the family are keen communists, there are lectures and meetings.

Week-ends are the real opportunity for leisure. In summer, there are sport and rambles in the country to pick berries. In winter, there is a chance to skate in the local park, and many families have their own skis and toboggans.

▲ The nomadic people of Central and Asiatic Russia live in tents made of skins. These can easily be moved from place to place.

▲ Many old wooden houses (called *izbas*) still remain, especially in villages. Three generations often live together.

▲ A modern living room in a Russian flat. Although conditions are very cramped, the family can now afford to buy clothes, furniture, toys and other luxuries.

▼ Many older houses, with their little patch of garden still survive, especially on the outskirts of the towns. Sunflowers are grown here for their seeds.

▲ In the old towns wood was often used to build big houses. Windows and doors are often decorated with ornamental patterns.

▲ In order to build houses quickly prefabricated parts are used. Television aerials are frequently to be seen.

▲ In every big town one sees huge blocks of flats, built on stock designs to help solve the serious housing problem.

A Moscovite family's day

For most Soviet people the day begins early. This family is lucky in having a grandmother, who looks after the house, while the mother and father are both at work. All the family have their lunch out, either in the works canteen, or restaurant. The mother is lucky if she only works part of the day, since she can then shop in the afternoon. Otherwise women take turns to give up their lunch hour to shop for everybody in the office. At five o'clock most people have finished work and go home for an evening's relaxation, though mother still has housework to do. This family is fortunate in the amount of space it has in its flat, though even here the children sleep in the living room.

Holidays and leisure

Leisure with a purpose

Soviet people take their pleasures seriously. They like to have an aim, even when spending the time which is entirely their own. It is difficult to imagine Russians going aimlessly for a walk in the country, though they might go to pick mushrooms or berries, to visit a place of historic importance, to walk twenty kilometres as a training exercise, or for a swim at the local beach.

A feature of Russian culture which excites admiration is the enjoyment of the arts. Quite ordinary people will talk, with obvious delight, about symphony concerts. There is nearly always a crowd at the door of the theatre clamouring for returned tickets.

Of course, the Soviet people are not always deadly serious. When they are happy, they are very cheerful and even boisterous. But popular entertainers get no encouragement to introduce vulgarity and violence.

Holidays in the sun

People in the Soviet Union now have far more leisure time, and more money, than ever before. It is therefore possible to spend the week-ends in many fresh ways, and to get away from home for a couple of days. Many people now have over 20 days holiday a year. This provides an opportunity for holidays in the country or at the seaside.

The role of the State

The State is concerned that people should enjoy their free time. Those who have worked well in their jobs, or for the Party, earn cheap fares and good accommodation at some of the best holiday resorts. For the millions of children between 10 and 15 who belong to the Young Pioneers, the State has provided camps with many exciting ways of spending holidays, and provided clubs, where members can spend their leisure time on a variety of hobbies.

▼ A narrow-gauge railway run by school children, under the watchful eye of expert engineers. There are similar miniature railways in the parks of many larger cities.

▲ A roundabout in the Gorky Park in Moscow. Parks of culture and leisure offer serious educational and cultural entertainment as well as amusements and sideshows.

◀ Automatic mineral water machines are a common sight in the towns.

▲ Games of chess in a public park. People take the game very seriously, and follow with a great deal of understanding the play of the world champions. Russia has produced some of the world's finest masters of the game. Dominoes, which demand less skill, are also popular.

▼ Spring at Pavlovsk, in Russia. The end of winter comes very suddenly, and the ice on the river breaks up. It is great fun, although very dangerous, to ride down the river on the ice floes.

◀ A beach on the river near Kiev. Such beaches, many miles from the sea, are common in Russia. Here citizens can relax, lying in the sun without travelling far from home. Beach holiday spots are found all over the warm south.

The super-sportsmen

The best of everything

In the Soviet Union there are no "professional" sportsmen, receiving wages for playing games. There are, however, great advantages in being a world-class athlete. The State provides them with the best equipment and coaching. They live in conditions which enable them to achieve their best. In some cases, if travelling is a problem, athletes live with their coach's family for much of the year. In return, they are expected to work hard, and acquire skills of the very highest order.

As a result, the Soviet Union is, with the United States, among the leading medal-winners in international events. Soviet sportsmen have always done well in sports which call for strength and stamina, such as weight-lifting, heavy-weight boxing, long-distance running and the field events, as well as some Nordic winter-sports. They have also astonished the world by the brilliance of their gymnasts and ice-skaters.

▲ Football is very popular among Soviet men and boys. The Soviet authorities give them active encouragement. Here they have put up a goal post on a deserted part of the beach, where players will not interfere with other people on the beach.

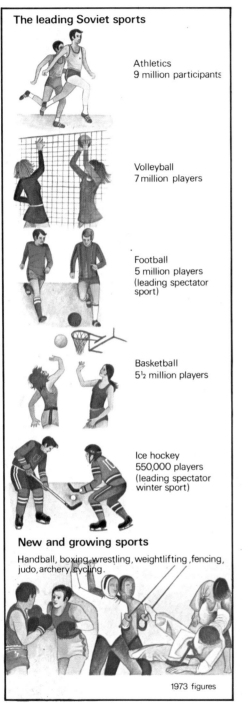

The leading Soviet sports

Athletics
9 million participants

Volleyball
7 million players

Football
5 million players
(leading spectator sport)

Basketball
5½ million players

Ice hockey
550,000 players
(leading spectator winter sport)

New and growing sports

Handball, boxing, wrestling, weightlifting, fencing, judo, archery, cycling.

1973 figures

▲ Sport plays a big part in the leisure of many people in the Soviet Union. The table shows the numbers of people who participate in regular sporting activities.

▶ Olga Korbut, the Soviet gymnast, in a brilliant performance on the high bars. She became a star at the Munich Olympics in 1972 with her charming and daring performances.

▼ Valerii Borzov (932) on his way to another victory. Borzov won the 100 and 200 metre events at Munich in 1972, and is one of the world's greatest sprinters. Soviet athletes generally are among the world's finest.

▲ An event in the World Student Games in the Lenin Stadium, Moscow. In swimming, as in every other sport, the Soviet Union can meet the highest international standards. This magnificent, well-equipped pool, was built especially for the games.

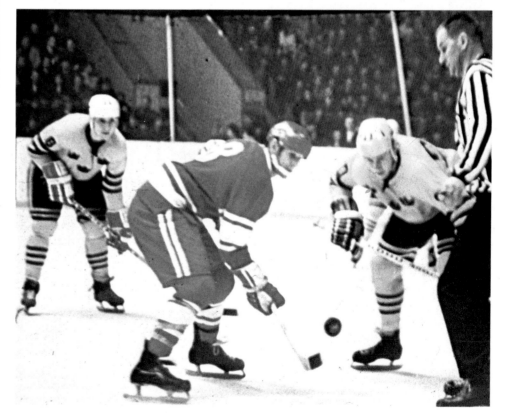

▲ Volleyball continues to grow in popularity in the Soviet Union. The great advantage is that it can be played almost anywhere, where there is space for a net.

▶ An ice-hockey match between the U.S.S.R. and Sweden. The newspaper *Izvestia* sponsored this competition.

The role of media

Newspapers for everyone

The two most important Russian newspapers are *Pravda* (Truth), the newspaper of the Communist Party, and *Izvestia* (News), the organ of the Trade Unions. Both have enormous circulations, and in March 1967 *Izvestia* set a world record for a daily paper with a total circulation of 8,670,000. They have even more readers. Nobody knows exactly how many people they reach, as copies are pasted up in prominent places where they can be read by anyone.

The Soviet Government plays a more direct role in communications than in most Western countries, where editors are employed by private owners of newspapers rather than the State. The State considers communication to have a serious purpose; as a result, papers contain less gossip and sensation, and more political and moral instruction. TASS, the news agency distributes items to newspapers at home and abroad. Items believed to be harmful to the national interest are censored.

Pravda and *Izvestia* are only two of scores of papers, published in many languages across the country. Not all are published in Moscow: some are published as far away as Vladivostok.

To Western readers, Soviet newspapers may seem dull. *Izvestia* may give up three of its four pages to speeches from the Congress of the Young Communists' League, with just a few items of general news on the back page! And the material looks different: there are no advertisements.

Publications in the Soviet Union are cheap, and there is a very wide variety of magazines for different groups. Some are published in English and other European languages. These are often attractively illustrated.

Radio and television

Radio and television now cover nearly every accessible part of the Union. Television is broadcast in black and white as well as colour and sets are now to be found in more than half the homes of the Soviet Union. Television, like the newspapers, carries no advertising.

morning

▲ The Soviet Union is the largest country in the world. It stretches across eleven time zones, and includes very many types of climate. This vast size, and the differences of

▲ A newspaper kiosk in Moscow. It sells a great variety of newspapers and magazines, many translated into European languages. It might be possible to buy a foreign newspaper from one of the Eastern bloc countries, but papers like the London *Times* or the U.S. *Wall Street Journal* are not stocked.

▶ A hall in the Exhibition of Economic Achievements, Moscow. This building, called the Kosmos hall, is devoted to the achievements of the Soviet Union in the exploration of space. Visiting exhibitions is a popular leisure activity, and helps to teach people about their country.

Sports programmes

▲ Television plays a big part in the lives of the Soviet people. Sports programmes are constant favourites. Some people have a set in the kitchen so as not to miss a programme while preparing a meal!

Cultural programmes

▲ Documentary programmes are popular; so are cultural programmes, particularly music, ballet and drama. The B.B.C.'s production of the *Forsyte Saga* was a great success when shown on Soviet television.

Communicating across eleven time zones and many natural barriers

afternoon

evening

climate, culture, race and language, make communication difficult. If a radio announcer in Moscow wanted to greet all the people with a bright good morning when it was 8 o'clock by his watch, he would reach people in the Far East at 6 o'clock in the evening ! Then his words would have to be translated into more than a hundred languages. In practice, bulletins are relayed from local centres, using material prepared by TASS, to overcome some of the problems of distance and time.

— Ты опять потерял ключи?
Рис. С. Ашмарина.

▲ "I suppose you have lost your keys again!" reads the caption. The Russian sense of humour is rather like that of the British.

▼ "Moscow and Leningrad compete" says the heading on this poster. It encourages the citizens of Moscow to increase their work efforts. This kind of friendly rivalry between cities is encouraged.

Cartoon programmes

▲ Soviet television has a number of special children's programmes, like the cartoon series shown here. These comic characters tell a moral tale through their escapades. Violence and obscenity are avoided.

A rigorous education

▲ A drawing lesson at Kindergarten. Children may go to such classes up to the age of seven, when formal education begins. There is a shortage of kindergarten schools.

The beginning of the school year

Early in September, after the long summer holidays, the Soviet Union school year begins. The pupils, often bringing flowers, are met at the gates by their teachers. Sometimes, there is a works' band from a local factory in the playground, playing cheerful tunes. It is a pleasant beginning to the year, but soon the serious work begins. School begins at around 8.30. Very young children finish about mid-day, but seniors continue until about 2.30. Schools are open for six days a week. In some towns, if there is a shortage of schools, or many parents work shifts, some pupils begin their day in the afternoon, and work until the evening.

Boys and girls are often taught together in the same class, and many of the teachers are women. Children are expected to go to the school nearest to their homes, and they normally remain there. Often they finish school with the same classmates that they met on the very first day.

Russian schools are usually built with a wide corridor on one side, and classrooms on the other. It is often too cold to go outside, and pupils spend their "breaks" in the corridor. There they can talk, and eat food bought from the canteen.

The emphasis on hard work

Schools are free (although parents may have to pay for textbooks), and everyone must go to school from the age of 7 until 15 or 16. The leaving age will soon be raised to 17. Even the youngest pupils do homework, and this increases to four hours a day for the seniors. Seniors must work hard if they wish to go to university: because education is free, there may be twenty applications for every place in the best universities.

After school

Education is not over when school finishes. Young children can join the "Octoberists" who wear little red stars. They have the motto. "Love your school, respect old people, and work hard". When they are 10, they may join the "Pioneers", and earn the right to wear the red neckscarf. The State provides many facilities for the Pioneers. Later still, they may join the "Komsomol". —the Young Communists' League. Even in later life, education continues. The Party and trade unions arrange functions to enable people to develop their work skills, or to learn an art or craft. The government hopes to raise people's standards of attainment, and to instil ideals of Communism.

The Soviet school system

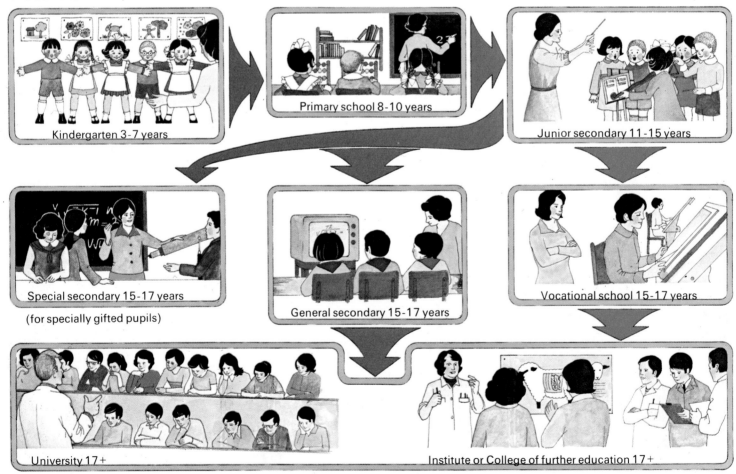

Kindergarten 3-7 years

Primary school 8-10 years

Junior secondary 11-15 years

Special secondary 15-17 years
(for specially gifted pupils)

General secondary 15-17 years

Vocational school 15-17 years

University 17+

Institute or College of further education 17+

▲ A senior teacher addresses her pupils in the courtyard at a school in Tblisi, Georgia. Many of the boys and girls have red scarves, which they have earned the right to wear as members of the Young Pioneers.

▼ Frilly aprons, like these, used to be worn by schoolgirls, to protect their brown school uniforms. Today aprons are seldom seen in the large centres, for schools also feel the influence of fashion.

▼ The many state universities provide free education to thousands of the ablest students, but it is sometimes difficult to obtain a place. The best universities only accept one out of twenty qualified applicants.

▲ A training ship for members of the Young Pioneers who are interested in seamanship. The Government of the U.S.S.R. sets aside a great deal of money to train young citizens, to enable them to lead useful and interesting lives.

23

Customs from many cultures

Grandfather Frost

▲ Grandfather Frost gives the little girl a present at the New Year. He looks very much like Father Christmas, although Christmas is not recognized. The words on his house mean "A happy New Year".

Christian festivals

Many customs in pre-Revolutionary Russia were linked to church festivals. The State no longer supports the churches, but they are crowded on the major holy days. Easter is the most important Christian festival, and people used to paint beautiful designs on eggs for the Easter feast. Occasionally, today, old women are seen, gathered outside a church waiting for the priest to bless their Easter cakes.

New Year's Day is a pleasant holiday, a non-religious Christmas. Children are given toys, and young ones treated to a visit to Grandfather Frost. Some families will also buy a tree for the house, and decorate it.

The coming of Spring

The coming of Spring means a great deal to Russians, and villagers in the north celebrate with a pancake feast and much jollity. The prettiest girl, dressed as Spring, may be given gifts of bread and salt by the Chairman of the Collective Farm, while another dressed as Winter, gets a going-away present of a jug of wine.

One thing which often strikes foreigners as strange is the practice of welcoming visitors—men and women—with bouquets of flowers. Another is the practice, when somebody is being applauded, for that person to join in the clapping. In fact, Russians see it as a way of showing their thanks to the audience.

◄ A group of musicians and dancers from Georgia in the south. They are wearing the traditional costume of the region. The best of these groups travel all over Russia and also abroad.

Baba Iaga—the witch

▲ Baba Iaga and her owl accomplice. Here Baba Iaga, the ugly witch, fails to catch the young girl she had been fattening up to eat because a river and a forest spring up to bar her way. The story is somewhat like the German fairy tale of *Hansel and Gretel*, though it seems crueller than the Grimm brothers' stories. Baba Iaga has terrified generations of Russian children. She is often shown with a crow or raven instead of an owl.

◄ May Day is one of the most important holidays in the Soviet Union. In many cities there are big parades of workers and the armed forces. The parades in Red Square, Moscow, are the most famous. The parade shown here is a typical one.

▼ An Easter service in the Novodevichii Monastery, Moscow. The altar is covered in pure gold. Although the State has no official religion, and leaders have tried hard to discredit the Christian churches, Russian Orthodox Christianity survives.

▼ A Russian circus. In the Soviet Union there are proper training schools for acrobats, clowns and other performers, and the standards are high. Even people who dislike circuses can enjoy such performances.

Heroes
of the people

▲ An unusual portrait of Lenin, made from plants of different colours. Lenin, the founder of the Soviet State, is the greatest of the Russian people's heroes.

▼ The celebrated writer, Maxim Gorky, being greeted by International Socialists during a visit to London in 1907. Gorky has been a Soviet hero for many years.

Heroes of the revolution

The Soviet people are constantly reminded of the leaders of the Revolution. Lenin, the greatest name of all, is remembered not only by countless statues and portraits, but by buildings and streets named after him. Petrograd (known earlier as St. Petersburg) was renamed Leningrad. The famous old town of Nijni-Novgorod is now called Gorky, and there are many other towns which have been renamed after heroes of the Revolution.

The folk-tales of Russia are full of stories of real people, whose actions have become more fanciful in the telling. Among them is Prince Igor, whose warlike exploits later became the subject of Borodin's opera. Prince Alexander Nevsky's heroism in battle against the Teutonic Knights later inspired Eisenstein to make one of the greatest of Russian films.

People who have fought against great odds to defend their homeland have always inspired writers. Tolstoi's great novel, *War and Peace*, is about Russia at the time of Napoleon's invasion. The "Order of Suvarov" an award for outstanding service in defence of the homeland, is named after the great Russian general of that period.

More recently, the exploits of thousands of partizans, who worked behind the German front-lines during the war have often been retold, and their memory kept fresh by statues and memorials.

▼ A Russian cosmonaut getting ready for his journey into space. Since Yuri Gagarin made the first ever space flight, the cosmonauts have been among the country's most popular adventurer heroes.

▲ Ivan Tsarevitch, the King's son, sets out on his marvellous adventures in search of a wife. Russian children still read with interest legends about the princes and princesses of pre-Revolutionary days.

▶ Monuments to the ordinary people who fought to bring about the revolution are very common all over the Soviet Union.

▼ Russian soldiers waiting to go into battle. This scene is from a production of Tolstoi's *War and Peace.* Napoleon's failure to hold Moscow in 1812 is one of the great epics of Russian history. Novels of the nineteenth century, like those of Tolstoi, are still widely read.

▼ The Babushka, or grandmother, who looks after the children while the parents are at work, is a much loved figure in Soviet life. But, today, in towns Babushkas are tending to find flats and jobs for themselves!

27

Shops and markets

▼ Soviet bank notes. In Russia 100 kopeks equals one rouble. There are notes worth 100, 50, 25, 10, 5, 3 and 1 rouble as well as coins for amounts up to 1 rouble. It is strictly forbidden to take Soviet coins out of the country. It is difficult to say how much a rouble is "worth" because the amount foreigners get for their pounds and dollars is fixed by the Government. Many prices in Russia are also controlled. Some commodities are very cheap and some very expensive.

Roubles — the basic unit of currency

1 rouble

3 roubles

5 roubles

10 roubles

25 roubles

State-owned shops

In the Soviet Union, shops belong to the State, and the people who work in them are paid wages by the Government. So one does not see the shopkeeper's name above the door, but simply "Central Delicatessen", "Meat", or "Books".

Since the State also controls the manufacture and supply of goods, no money is spent for advertisements on hoardings, television and in the newspapers, telling people about one brand or another. Shops are better stocked than they were. Even so, shortages do still occur. This is usually because the system of distribution has failed, and people often feel that officials in charge of distribution do not take enough notice of what they really want. One difficulty, if one buys anything bulky, lies in getting it home, since there is no delivery service. Sometimes people take furniture home on a barrow.

Many shops, and the goods they sell, strike foreigners as rather old-fashioned. However, some of the bigger places have food supermarkets, and there are a few shops selling prepared foodstuffs.

Even so, shopping in the Soviet Union is rather a tedious business. It is particularly hard on women, who must give up their lunch-hour to shop. Sometimes women take turns to buy for their colleagues, so that perhaps their turn comes only once a week.

Many shops use accounting machines, but some still use the abacus (a sort of bead frame) to work out the bill. It is surprising how well it works!

The triple queue system

Stage 1, select the goods and receive a docket

▲ In the bigger Russian shops, the assistant who serves does not take the money. Since there are often many customers at the counter, this means joining three queues: to get served, to pay for the goods, and then to collect them. This can make shopping very tedious.

▲ A free market, near Moscow. Peasants have been allowed to keep a small piece of ground around their houses and they are allowed to sell any surplus vegetables they grow. Some surpluses from the State farms are also sold in this way. These stalls are very popular because the goods are fresher than in the State shops, but prices are higher.

Stage 2, pay the cashier

Stage 3, receive the purchases

▲ This fine baker's and confectioner's in Gorky Street, Moscow, dates from before the Revolution. In such shops it is sometimes possible to buy a glass of chocolate to drink, while eating the cake one has just bought.

▲ Russians buy a great many books and queues often form outside a bookshop if a particularly important work has been published. Many books are published at prices which nearly everybody can afford. Children's books are often well produced and beautifully illustrated.

◄ The famous State International Store (G.U.M.) in Red Square, Moscow. It is really a shopping arcade on two floors, with many small shops in the bays. On the third floor, which can be seen in the far distance, are the workshops of the tailors and dressmakers.

Soviet cooking and eating

Daily fare of working people

In the days before the Revolution, the Russians invented some wonderful dishes; but fine cooking demands money, leisure and an abundant supply of the right ingredients. It is most likely to be found among émigré families and in expensive Russian restaurants abroad. The visitor is not likely to find it in most hotels and restaurants, where meals are large, filling, and often rather greasy. Many people have a quick breakfast, a large snack to eat mid-morning, a canteen lunch, and, for supper, whatever can be obtained during a quick visit to the shops at lunchtime.

The position is constantly improving. A number of shops selling ready-prepared dishes are appearing in the big cities. There are also some expensive, yet well-patronized restaurants. But they are less likely to serve typically Russian food than dishes from Georgia and other regions of the Soviet Union. Southern republics, including Georgia, have dishes similar to some from Turkey and Greece. Kebabs are an example.

The Soviet people are hospitable, and guests invited for a meal will find a loaded table. In Russia, pickled herring with a little salad, or caviar may be followed by *shchi* (cabbage soup) or *borshch* (beetroot soup)—both meals in themselves—then a main course of meat or fish. The wines of the Soviet Union are also excellent. The meal could end with drinks of vodka—or with pastries and tea.

▲ Delicious pastries from market stalls are often bought to eat at home.

Make yourself a Russian meal

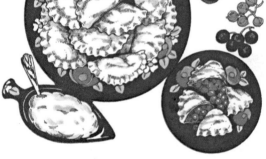

BORSHCH (BEETROOT SOUP)
⅓ oz. butter
¾ oz. chopped onions
½ lb. beetroot, peeled and cut small
1 tablespoon wine vinegar
1 tomato, roughly chopped
½ teaspoon salt, little pepper
1 pint beef stock
¼ lb. white cabbage (shredded)
¼ lb. cooked brisket (cut up)
1 oz. frankfurter sausages (cut up)
parsley and a piece of bay leaf
sour cream to serve with soup

Melt butter in saucepan. Add onions and cook till soft. Add beetroot and other ingredients (except cabbage, meat, parsley, bay leaf and some of the beef stock). Simmer for 50 minutes. Add rest of stock with cabbage and bring to boil. Add meat and tied stalks of parsley and bay leaf. Cook for half an hour. Taste constantly and remove the herb when the flavour is strong enough. Salt to taste. Serve with a tub of sour cream.

BEEF STROGANOV
½ lb. fillet of beef (without fat) cut in small strips
¼ lb. sliced onions
¼ lb. mushrooms
good ½ teaspoon of mustard
½ teaspoon sugar
½ teaspoon salt, pepper to taste
1 tablespoon vegetable cooking oil

Mix mustard, sugar and salt into a thick paste and leave for at least 15 minutes.

Heat some of the oil and cook the vegetables until soft. Drain off the oil and stand on one side. Take another pan and heat the remainder of the oil till very hot. Cook the meat for a few minutes, turning constantly. Transfer the cooked meat into the pan with vegetables and simmer them together (adding a little more oil if necessary). Stir in sour cream with mustard, salt and sugar, being careful that the cream does not curdle. Simmer for few minutes, then serve with straw potatoes (chips).

VARENYKY
(Sweet dumplings filled with cherries)

Dough
4 oz. plain flour
1 egg and 1 beaten egg white
3 tablespoons milk
little salt
Mix till dough is stiff enough to form a ball. Add a little milk if necessary. Dust with flour and chill for 30 minutes.

Cherries
8 oz. drained sour cherries
1 oz. sugar (or to taste)
Simmer in pan till cherries are soft and sugar melted. Roll out dough and press out circles with a wide-rimmed glass. Coat with beaten egg-white. Put cherries in circle and fold over, pressing edges to seal. Bring pan of water to boil, let dumplings simmer for about ten minutes until they float. Transfer to heated dish. On serving moisten with melted butter. Serve with cherry sauce and sweet cream.

A typical day's menu

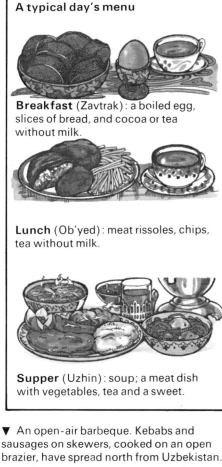

Breakfast (Zavtrak): a boiled egg, slices of bread, and cocoa or tea without milk.

Lunch (Ob'yed): meat rissoles, chips, tea without milk.

Supper (Uzhin): soup; a meat dish with vegetables, tea and a sweet.

▲ A small self-service restaurant. A high degree of cleanliness is maintained and the staff wear head-scarves and overalls.

Some famous traditional dishes

▼ An open-air barbeque. Kebabs and sausages on skewers, cooked on an open brazier, have spread north from Uzbekistan.

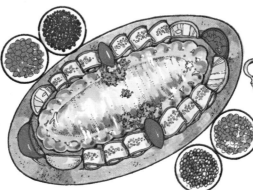

▲ Sturgeon in aspic, dressed with cucumber, lemon and tomato, with side-dishes of different kinds of caviar. There are at least eight kinds of caviar. Caviar is made from the roe of the sturgeon.

▲ Pancakes like bliny are eaten with many side dishes, butter and sour cream. The samovar, seen on the left, is used to water down the strong tea, and to keep the pot warm.

▲ Chicken Kiev with a side-dish of salad. The boned chicken breast is folded over a piece of butter and chilled before being rolled in crumbs and fried in deep fat.

▲ Gozinakh and Klava. These are sweet-meats from the south similar to Greek and Turkish sweets, and equally delicious. Nuts and honey are important ingredients.

31

Moscow heart of Russia

The wooden fortress

Moscow is not an ancient city. When it was first mentioned, in 1147 A.D., it was little more than a village. A few years later, Prince Yuri Dolgoruky had a wooden fortress built on a nearby hill, overlooking the Moscow River. After a time, this was replaced by stone walls. Then, between 1485–95, the brick walls, which now enclose the area known as the Kremlin, were built. Moscow had by that time so far outdistanced ancient rivals like Novgorod and Vladimir that it had become the chief city of a growing Empire. It remained the capital until 1703, when Peter the Great moved his court to St. Petersburg (now called Leningrad). In 1918, after the Revolution, Moscow again became the capital.

Old Moscow has been rapidly disappearing as new blocks of flats and offices, broad avenues and spacious squares have been constructed; but in the back streets it is still possible to find the wooden houses of old Moscow and the mansions of the former aristocrats and merchants. The State has been careful to preserve the best of these historic buildings.

The Kremlin

Moscow is planned like a spider's web within two great circular thoroughfares—the Boulevard Ring and the Sadovoye Ring. At the centre is the Kremlin. Within its walls are the official residences of the Heads of State, the Palace of Congresses, the Palace of the Czars, and several cathedrals with their treasures.

Along one side of the Kremlin walls is Red Square. This is the central point of parades when thousands of workers and soldiers march in procession. The parades also provide the opportunity to display rockets and other new developments in defence. The tomb of Lenin is also in Red Square.

No visit to Moscow is complete without a journey on its famous underground railway —perhaps to visit the Exhibition of Economic Achievements, or to Moscow's University on the Lenin Hills.

Things to see in Moscow

1. The Spasskaya Gate, the main gate into the Kremlin.
2. The Czar's Cannon. The biggest calibre gun in the world, it weighs 40 tons.
3. The Cathedral of the Assumption is one of the four Kremlin cathedrals.
4. The building of the Moscow City Soviet.

▲ The cathedral of St. Basil, Moscow was built for Czar Ivan the Terrible between 1555 and 1561, to commemorate his military success at Kazan. He is said to have had the architects blinded so that they could never create another church as beautiful.

▼ New Moscow, a view along the river showing new buildings and roads. The broad embankment along the River Moskva has room for eight rows of cars! The space between the lines in the middle is reserved for ambulances, the police, and government cars.

▲ The Iverskia Gate, Moscow in 1910. This used to be one of the entrances into Red Square but was pulled down to make it easier for processions and military vehicles to enter the square. Red Square was called by that name before the Revolution, and though some changes have been made, it still has the outlines of old Moscow.

◄ 1917-1967: Moscow commemorates in lights the fiftieth anniversary of the Revolution. The event was the occasion for great rejoicing in the Soviet Union, and Moscow showed its gayest and brightest face. Moscow, the capital of the whole Soviet Union, is the focus of national celebrations.

▼ The People's Friendship fountain in the grounds of the National Economic Achievements Exhibition, Moscow. The fifteen figures represent the fifteen republics of the Soviet Union. This huge exhibition occupies 500 acres outside of Moscow.

Ballet Russe

A great national art

Ballet is an art the Soviet people take very seriously. The famous Moscow Bolshoi and Leningrad Kirov are only two of the 36 important ballet companies.

The first Russian ballet was performed in 1742 at the coronation of Peter the Great's daughter. Early development was slow. Nearly everywhere, the ballet was a pretext to display fine costumes and jewellery. Only in St. Petersburg and Moscow was ballet treated as an art.

Russians have a natural talent for dancing—it has been said that Russians dance as Italians sing and birds fly—and in the early 1900s some Russians began to feel that dancing should be more expressive of the emotions and should be made to interpret some of the fine music available. Moreover, a ballet should be one continuous whole, and not a set of separate dances. Mikhail Fokine and Aleksandr Benois were among the leaders who joined Diaghilev in France, and, in 1909, Diaghilev's *Ballet russe* took Paris by storm. Before long, the names of such dancers as Anna Pavlova and Nijinsky were world famous. The composer, Igor Stravinsky, also wrote some exciting scores for Diaghilev. By 1917, the Russian ballet was pre-eminent.

After the Revolution

After the Revolution, the Russian leaders were of two minds about the ballet, mainly because it has always been connected with the court of the Czars. Fortunately, Lenin decided to give it his support.

Like every other form of art, the Ballet felt the heavy hand of Stalin. Dancers and composers were instructed to "liquidate their anti-people practices". The result was that the 1930s and 1940s produced little of importance apart from *Romeo and Juliet* with music by Prokofiev. Today, Russian ballet is once more developing.

The beginner admitted to the Bolshoi school will receive not only strict training, but the best rehearsal conditions and facilities. The members of the ballet company are well-paid. Above all, they know that they are performing before a knowledgeable and appreciative audience.

▲ The Bolshoi theatre, Moscow. is one of the world's great theatres. The building only dates from 1856, but the walls and portico belong to an earlier building which was destroyed by fire. Apart from productions on its main stage, the company also travels and performs in the Palace of Congresses, before audiences of 6,000.

▼ Scene from *Swan Lake* at the Bolshoi. It is often performed at the Bolshoi theatre. The standard is so high that dancers must have years of experience before taking leading roles. At the same time, the Bolshoi is criticized for being unadventurous, in failing to perform new ballets and preferring classics like *Swan Lake*.

◀ A pair of dancers from the Georgian State Ballet Company. Their principal theatre in Tbilisi is world famous. During the centuries when the Georgians were ruled by foreign powers, they clung to their old dances as a means of national expression. The finest of these old dances is *Simd*, an Ossetian wedding dance. In many of the old dances there are links with Indian folk-dance. Much of the Company's high reputation is due to the creative ability of the husband and wife team who head the group.

▲ A Moscow folk dance in regional costume. Each region has its dances, which appreciative audiences help to keep alive. They are often accompanied by an accordion player. Some of the orchestra are holding three-cornered balalaikas.

▼ An Armenian Dance Company, from Yerevan. They are wearing the traditional costumes of this part of the country. The dancing of the south is marked by the remarkable agility of the men dancers.

▼ Some old folk tales tell of heroes devastating invaders. These nineteenth century illustrations show the influence of Russian dancing, in the movement of the figures. In this way, artistry is lent to violence.

Arts
ancient and new

◀ An icon of St. George, formerly the patron saint of Moscow. At one time, such religious paintings, with a light burning before them, were to be found in many Russian homes. This type of painting helps to show the close link between the Russian and Greek churches.

▼ The Cathedral of the Assumption, Moscow was built in the fifteenth century as the private church of the Czars. Commoners were also allowed to attend services there. When Napoleon captured the Kremlin he turned it into a stable, and his troops pillaged the treasures of the cathedral. It is now a museum. Its architecture is characteristic of medieval Russia and Kiev with its onion-shaped golden domes topped by golden crosses.

State support for the arts

Since the Revolution, the Soviet Government has done much to broaden the cultural life of ordinary people. Great sums of money have been spent on building concert halls, art galleries and parks of "culture and leisure". Concerts, art exhibitions and poetry readings have been promoted. And artists whose work has found favour have been paid well. Russian people—even people with little education—have a rich enjoyment of the arts. Popular poets have even found sports stadiums packed to hear them read their works.

The Soviet Union, however, differs from the West in the control which it exercises over the work of artists and writers. Even the most trifling pieces of literature must be submitted for approval. Some writers, who know that their work will not meet with approval, circulate writings typed on thin paper among their friends, and occasionally books are smuggled abroad for publication.

Recent developments

Some outstanding books have been written in spite of the censorship. Some writers whose natural bent is towards socialism and who take an optimistic view of social progress, have not been affected by it. But Boris Pasternak was not able to have his most famous novel, *Doctor Zhivago*, published at home.

Changes of policy can make life difficult for writers. At one time Solzhenitsyn was allowed to publish *A Day in the Life of Ivan Denisovich*, a story about life in Stalin's prison camps!

The State's claim to decide what is good art and what is bad has weighed heavily upon painters and sculptors. In 1974, however, a number of artists decided to show their work in a field outside Moscow. There was an outcry when their first show was broken up, and a second show was allowed. In recent years, there have been some notable constructions—including the great Hall of Congresses in the Kremlin and the monument to space achievement—which incorporated newer ideals.

▲ Aram Khachaturian (b. 1903), the great Armenian composer, conducts a symphony orchestra. The "Sabre Dance" is his most popular work, and he has made excellent use of Armenian folk tunes. Symphony concerts draw big crowds in Russia, and the standard of local State orchestras is very high. Music is one of the Soviet Union's most popular arts. Many great composers have come from Russia (Tchaikovsky, Rimsky Korsakov, and Rachmaninov, for example), and some of the Soviet Republics have a rich heritage of folk music.

▶ The monument, "The Conquest of Space", in the grounds of the National Economic Achievements Exhibition, Moscow. It represents a rocket leaving a long vapour trail behind it. As a work of art, it has been widely admired.

▼ A scene, depicting the retreat from Moscow, in the Soviet film of Tolstoi's *War and Peace*. Russian producers have made some great films in the past fifty years. Eisenstein, an early film producer, began this tradition.

▲ Feodor Dostoievsky (1812-81) was one of the most brilliant novelists of the nineteenth century. Dostoievsky's novels are at once tragic and humorous. Like Dickens (whom he admired) his novels are packed with observations on life and character. Dostoievsky was very conscious of the dark side of the human mind, and aware that many aspirations are destined to fail.

Transport for a vast land

Some traditional forms of transport

▲ The horse-drawn sledge is still used in villages in winter. The three-horse sledge is called a "troika"

▲ In Tashkent, transport is often still primitive, with the donkey as the beast of burden, often carrying very heavy loads.

▲ In Turkmenia, and the arid southern regions of the Soviet Union, the camel is to be seen, carrying loads of cotton and other produce.

▼ A collection of bus and tram tickets from Moscow and Leningrad. Travel by bus and tram is very cheap in Russia.

▲ The *Lenin* is the world's biggest ice-breaker and the first atomic-powered ship. It was launched in Leningrad in 1957. The Soviet government is planning an even bigger ship which will break ice up to two metres (seven feet) thick. Ports in the north, and some of the rivers, are frozen for months. Ice-breakers can extend the shipping season by clearing a passage for shipping.

▶ A tram terminus near Moscow University. Most of the drivers are women, and there are no conductors. Travellers usually buy books of 3-kopek tickets, or drop the money into an automatic machine and then take a ticket. Since travellers are largely on their honour to pay their fare, it is considered very mean to travel without paying.

The pioneering role of railway

In many parts of the old Russian Empire, there were no roads. The coming of the railways was, therefore, an event of great importance. The Trans-Siberian Railway, built between 1891 and 1917, made it possible to develop Siberia. Today, the railway carries two-thirds of the goods and half of all passengers.

In early days, Russia's many great rivers were the principal way of moving people and goods. Unfortunately many flow into the Arctic or into inland seas, and most of them follow north-south courses while the movement of traffic is from east to west. As a result, except for the rivers of western Russia, their use is limited. Canals, and especially the canal system centred upon the Volga, have increased the use of some rivers, and made Moscow a "port of five seas". The Soviet Union has a coastline of 50,000 kilometres (30,000 miles), but much of it is liable to become frozen, so coastal shipping is of less importance.

The establishment of the State airline, Aeroflot, in 1923 was an event of significance. Today, it is the biggest airline in the world, and in 1972 carried 80 million passengers to 57 countries. There is a keen competition to see whether Aeroflot will have the first supersonic liner.

A big contribution is made by the gas and oil pipelines extending into Eastern Europe, and by the long-distance transmission of electricity. This spares the railways much heavy freight.

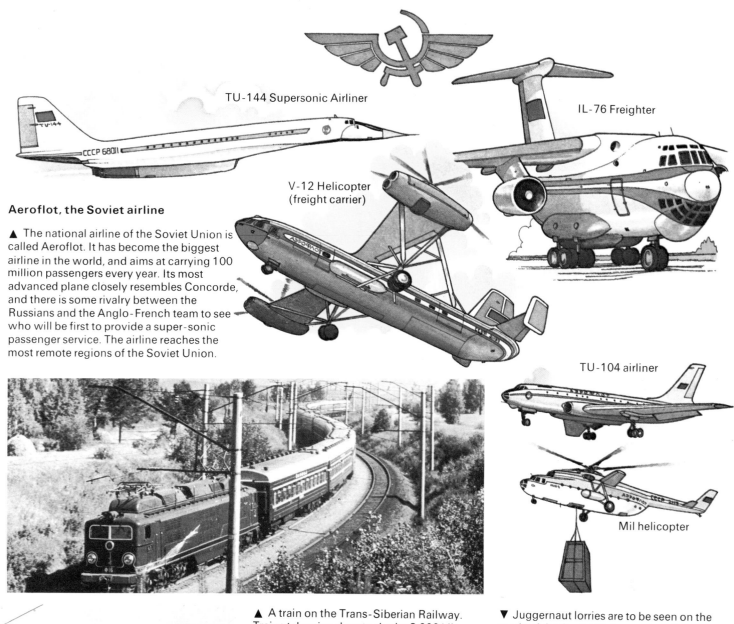

TU-144 Supersonic Airliner

IL-76 Freighter

V-12 Helicopter
(freight carrier)

Aeroflot, the Soviet airline

▲ The national airline of the Soviet Union is called Aeroflot. It has become the biggest airline in the world, and aims at carrying 100 million passengers every year. Its most advanced plane closely resembles Concorde, and there is some rivalry between the Russians and the Anglo-French team to see who will be first to provide a super-sonic passenger service. The airline reaches the most remote regions of the Soviet Union.

TU-104 airliner

Mil helicopter

▲ A train on the Trans-Siberian Railway. Trains take nine days to do the 8,000 kilometre (5,000 miles) journey from Moscow to Vladivostok. The railway was begun in 1891, and only completed in 1917. It has been tremendously important in the development of Siberia and the Far East.

▼ Juggernaut lorries are to be seen on the roads of the Soviet Union as elsewhere in Europe. This lorry carries goods between Moscow and Bulgaria. Lorries are taking over, in some areas, from the barges. Road transport is faster, but uses more fuel than canal and river transport.

Great Romanovs Peter and Catherine

▲ Peter realized that Russia could learn much from the West. As a young man he set off to visit and work in the shipyards of Holland and England.

▼ Battle of Lesna (1708) between Peter the Great and the Swedish forces of Charles XII. Peter was determined to acquire Swedish land to give Russia a port on the Baltic sea. Charles attempted to strike at Moscow, but was defeated at Poltava.

Peter the Great

When Peter came to the throne at the age of ten, in 1692, the Court was a crude and violent place. His position was not certain, and, while his stepsister ruled as Regent, Peter was sent to live outside Moscow.

These were among the happiest days of his life. He learned many useful things, but above all, he learned about Western Europe from the foreign workmen on the estate. He developed a great, even exaggerated, admiration for the West.

In 1697, now Czar Peter I, he set out to study in Holland and England. Trouble at home called him back. He restored order mercilessly, and then set about building a new army.

Peter's great rival was Charles XII of Sweden. His first campaign against Charles ended in disaster. Luckily for Peter, while he built his new capital, St. Petersburg, and strengthened the army, Charles wasted his time. When they met again, the Swedes were crushed. The war dragged on for ten years, but Russia had established herself on the Baltic four years before Peter's death, at the age of 43, in 1725.

Peter's plans were basically sensible, but they cost huge sums of money and caused untold misery. His worst error however, was that he split Russian society in two: he created a small aristocracy, which looked to the West for inspiration and had little to do with the culture of the mass of the people. It took the Revolution of 1917 to alter that.

Catherine the Great

Catherine II (1762–96) was the greatest Russian ruler after Peter the Great. She was a German by birth, and succeeded to the throne after the death of her husband, Czar Peter III. Like Peter the Great, she was shocked by the backwardness of Russia, and like him she had great admiration for the West. During her reign, French and not Russian, was spoken at Court, and the nobles were encouraged to read French literature.

She thought it a disgrace that Russia's peasant were serfs, yet during her reign their condition became worse.

Whereas Peter had forced his way to the Baltic, Catherine resolved to extend Russian power in the Black Sea area, and fought a victorious war against Turkey. Although she was obliged to give up these conquests, because the Austrians were alarmed, she took a piece of Poland instead.

The French Revolution

One particular sorrow of Catherine's life was the outbreak of the French Revolution in 1789. Her friendship with Voltaire and other French thinkers had not prepared her for such a dramatic turn of events. However, she refused to be drawn into the war against France, preferring instead to take advantage of any weakness in Poland or elsewhere in Eastern Europe. Catherine, while holding liberal views, was far from liberal in her foreign policy.

The Russian empire expands through Peter's conquests

Russian territory 1689
Russian gains 1721
Charles XII attack lines
Russian boundary 1725

▲ Peter's greatest enemy was Charles XII. In the beginning of the long war the Swedes were very successful and Peter was defeated at Narva. But Charles over-reached himself and Peter's new capital, St. Petersburg, built on Charles's land, was secured.

▼ The famous bronze statue of Peter in Leningrad, which he founded (as St. Petersburg) to become the new capital of Russia. The capital was moved back to Moscow after 1917.

▲ Catherine the Great (1762-96), the greatest ruler since Peter, was also anxious to develop Russia on Western lines, and like him wanted to make Russia strong in the West.

▼ Peter compelled the nobility to study something practical. Those who did not finish their courses were not allowed to marry!

▲ Peter regarded traditional dress as a symbol of backwardness. He put a tax on beards and sometimes cut them off himself.

▲ He weakened the power of the church by setting up a new ruling body answerable to the State. Nuns and monks were made to do useful work in the world.

▲ The position of the lowest classes, the serfs, became harder under Peter. Thousands lost their lives building Peter's new capital, St. Petersburg.

Lenin
the statemaker

The thinker and revolutionary

Lenin—his real name was Vladimir Ilyich Ulyanov—is the greatest figure in the history of the Russian Revolution.

He was born in a town on the Volga. Lenin and his brothers and sisters were all revolutionaries. He was already involved in revolutionary politics as a student. By 1894, he had given up his job to write and to teach revolutionary groups. In 1897 he was banished to Siberia for three years, and after that he lived much of his life, until 1917, abroad.

Had Lenin died before 1917, few people would have heard of him, in spite of his many writings. The revolutionary groups were divided among themselves and although Lenin's group called themselves the Bolsheviks (the big group), they were fewer in numbers, than the Mensheviks (the little group)! Lenin's great opportunity came in 1917. He was then hiding in Switzerland. For Russia, events in World War I were going badly, and a revolution in February 1917 had led the Czar to abdicate in favour of a liberal Government. Lenin returned to lead the Bolsheviks. Lenin would have no dealings with the liberals, who had become unpopular by trying to continue the war against Germany. He had, moreover, support among the Fleet and the Red Guard factory workers. On October 25–6, 1917, the Government was overthrown and the Bolsheviks came to power. Lenin sent Trotsky to make peace with Germany. The Kaiser was in a powerful position, and dictated harsh terms.

After the Revolution

There followed a period of hope for millions of Russians, but also a period of appalling difficulty. Industrial production fell, the country was invaded by foreign troops, and civil war broke out. In the countryside, millions died of starvation. To meet some of the troubles, Lenin's New Economic Policy allowed some free enterprise and he was forced to make concessions in framing the new Constitution. But Lenin was already a sick man and he died on January 21, 1924.

▲ Lenin in his study at the Kremlin. He is reading a copy of *Pravda*. In retrospect, Lenin's life was a triumph of achievement. Yet during his lifetime, his troubles outnumbered his successes.

◀ Czar Nicholas (1894-1918) with his wife Alexandra Fyodorovna. They were imprisoned with their children at the outbreak of the Revolution, and later murdered. Nicholas was a gentle man, though weak, and he never understood the dreadful problems of Russia. He had many failures—he was defeated by Japan, and unable to control the country In the First World War his troops were no match for the German army.

▼ "Bloody Sunday", January 22, 1905. The demonstration of Father Gapon was peaceful in intention. Workers thought that all would be well if they could talk with the Czar. Then they were met by troops, who opened fire on the helpless demonstrators, and killed many of them.

► The Russian cavalry has German foot-soldiers on the run, in this romanticized view of a battle in the First World War. In fact, the Russian army was no match for the well-disciplined, well-armed Germans, and Russian casualties were extremely heavy. After the Revolution of February 1917, the Czar abdicated and, after the October Revolution, Russia withdrew from a war she was in no condition to fight.

▼ The cruiser Aurora, which gave the signal for the start of the Revolution in October 1917. It is preserved at Leningrad.

▲ Lenin addresses a meeting of troops and workers in Petrograd. After successfully launching the Revolution, Lenin worked tirelessly to achieve a socialist state. He was a gifted speaker, who could inspire an audience. Here, he speaks under the flag of the Bolsheviks, the Red flag which is still the symbol of Leninist socialism. In the early days of Lenin's rule, Russia was still subject to unrest and upheaval.

► At first, it seemed that Lenin's Government would not survive. Lenin had made an expensive peace with Germany, and many people within the country were opposed to the Bolsheviks. Soon the dissident groups formed so-called "White Armies" and engaged in civil war. Here soldiers of the Red Army crowd onto the roof of a train, so bad was transport. By 1920 the White Armies had been defeated, and peace restored.

43

Stalin
man of steel

Stalin in power

It was Lenin's wish that Trotsky should succeed him. For another of his Ministers—Joseph Stalin (1897–1953)—he had nothing but loathing. Lenin, however, became ill before he could settle matters and Stalin cunningly gained control.

Stalin was not bothered with doubts about Communist ideals. He set about making Russia a great industrial Power. Factories, power-stations and steelworks were built, and tight production targets set. Stalin replaced the peasants' holdings by huge collective farms. Those who opposed were sent to prison camps. Farming regions which did not produce enough were starved into submission.

Khrushchev and the thaw

Stalin's death in 1953 brought great relief, but the scale of his atrocities was not known until 1956 when Nikita Khruschchev, the man who later became the Russian leader, denounced Stalin. Life in Russia then became much more tolerable.

Khrushchev, however, made political and economic mistakes, and was dismissed in 1964. Although his successors discontinued Khrushchev's liberal policy, the Soviet Union no longer suffers the terror of Stalin's day.

▲ Lenin with Stalin. Lenin greatly distrusted Stalin and tried to prevent him succeeding to the leadership of the Party. Stalin cleverly kept out of trouble by remaining in the background while Lenin was alive.

◄ Leon Trotsky (1879-1940) was the ablest writer and speaker among the early Revolutionaries. He was a friend of Lenin, but felt that the ideas of Lenin's group would lead to dictatorship. Trotsky became a member of the Communist government and was expected to succeed Lenin. But Stalin outwitted him and drove him into exile.

▼ The battle for Stalingrad 1942-3. After Hitler's surprise attack upon the Soviet Union, large areas were quickly overrun. The turning point was reached at Stalingrad in February 1943, when the Germans were halted, and gradually driven back.

Stalin's programme of modernization

▲ Stalin rids himself of his opponents. The most important was Trotsky. Trotsky was first demoted to unimportant jobs, and then sent into exile.

▲ Stalin did not build a real iron curtain round Russia, but by preventing contact between East and West, he sealed Russians off from the outside world.

▲ Stalin understood that the Soviet Union could only become a great power through rapid industrialization. He achieved this at great speed, but at heavy cost in human terms. Peasants were compelled to work long hours under bad conditions in the new factories.

▲ To get rid of the millions of smallholdings and to destroy the power of richer peasants, Stalin amalgamated small farms into large collective farms. In this way he hoped to get cheaper food for the towns. At first, there were dreadful famines in the countryside. The level of productivity on the farms declined, and there was much discontent among people on the land.

▲ Throughout Stalin's dictatorship his colleagues and even ordinary people lived in fear of arrest. There were repeated "purges", and many people who didn't fit in with Stalin's policies were sent to labour camps in Siberia.

▲ Women in Leningrad during the siege. During World War Two this city was nearly encircled by German troops for 900 days. In January 1944, the Red Army drove the Germans back. The people refused to surrender despite the most terrible conditions. These women, carrying their few possessions, had been made homeless by the bombardment.

▶ Khrushchev (third from the right) standing between Foreign Minister Molotov and Nikolai Bulganin with whom he temporarily shared power. After Stalin's death, his successors broke with Stalinist policies and denounced what he had done. Life in Russia became more pleasant and it seemed that understanding and trust between East and West might be possible.

The multi-nation

Languages and customs

Within the Soviet Union there are peoples of about 150 different nationalities. There are around the same number of languages, sometimes written in completely different scripts. These peoples are often of widely different origins, with different temperaments and racial characteristics. And, according to where they live—in the extreme north like the Eskimos or the south like the Armenians—they differ in their costume and way of life.

By far the largest group, making up more than half the population, are the Russians. Near neighbours in the west, with some differences of languages and culture, are the Ukrainians and the Byelorussians (White Russians). In the western part of the Soviet Union, too, there are about ten million European people, who are not Slavs like the Russians. They include the Lithuanians, Latvians, Estonians and Moldavians. They have their own history and culture. There are also people of Greek, Polish, and German origin. They follow their own way of life, but do not have their own national area. Jews have also played an important part in society. A national home has been created for them in the Birobidzhan Autonomous Region on the Chinese border, north of Vladivostok. Few people have a chance to visit this remote area and it is impossible to know how the scheme is working.

The peoples of the Soviet Union are encouraged to protect their own cultures, although their religions are discouraged. They are given considerable freedom to manage their own internal affairs through their own governments. Russians, however, dominate Soviet affairs, and the Russian language, which all children must learn, is the great unifying force.

▲ A group of Russians queue to buy ice-cream in a park near Moscow University underground station. In costume and appearance they have much in common with their close European neighbours, the Poles, the Czechs and the East Germans.

◄ Ukranian mother with her children on their way to a celebration. The children are wearing Ukranian national costumes. These are painstakingly embroidered by hand to traditional designs and are only worn on special occasions.

▲ A street scene in Tashkent, in the south of the Soviet Union, and the capital of Uzbekistan. The people here, and their way of life, are totally different from that in Moscow. The men are sitting on day-beds in a park drinking tea.

The Soviet nationalities, and where they live

▼ As the map shows, the majority of the population lives in the western half of the Soviet Union. Russians are easily the largest group and they live, not only in Russia itself, but scattered throughout the land.

White Russians (from the far west) are more often known as Byelorussians. The areas marked in pale green are very thinly populated desert lands in northern Siberia and near the Caspian Sea.

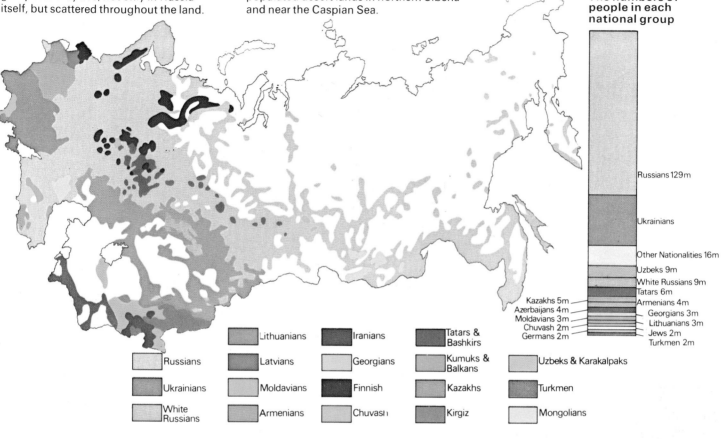

The numbers of people in each national group

Russians 129m
Ukrainians
Other Nationalities 16m
Uzbeks 9m
White Russians 9m
Tatars 6m
Armenians 4m
Kazakhs 5m
Azerbaijans 4m
Moldavians 3m
Chuvash 2m
Germans 2m
Georgians 3m
Lithuanians 3m
Jews 2m
Turkmen 2m

Russians
Ukrainians
White Russians

Lithuanians
Latvians
Moldavians
Armenians

Iranians
Georgians
Finnish
Chuvash

Tatars & Bashkirs
Kumuks & Balkans
Kazakhs
Kirgiz

Uzbeks & Karakalpaks
Turkmen
Mongolians

Some national costumes

◄ There are many different styles of dress in the Soviet Union, as one might expect from a land with such a range of climate and so many cultural differences. People within the Arctic Circle still wear heavy hooded anoraks made from fleecy skins, though they would wear shirts and trousers underneath. The costumes shown here come from the European part of the land. Their styles date from pre-revolutionary times, and they are only worn on special occasions.

Cossack the Urals

Voronezh Province

Nijni Novgorod Province

Tambov Province

Vereya Moscow Province

Travelling costumes Central Russia

Products of a world power

Creating an industrial nation

Since 1917, the Soviet Union has been transformed from a country where agriculture was of chief importance into one of the world's greatest industrial nations. This rapid change was possible because the State owned every industrial enterprise. Committees were set up in Moscow and the regions, and Plans—usually covering five years—were prepared. The first aim was to produce more coal, iron-ore and other materials; to build steel mills and factories for heavy industry; and to build railways and lines of communication. The country was to become self-sufficient.

Fortunately, the Soviet Union possesses nearly every raw material in great abundance. It has the world's biggest forests. It is rich in coal, iron-ore, manganese (used in steel-making), copper, zinc and lead, and new finds are constantly being made.

Russia also had workers, and the workforce was increased by women. Women still do heavy work. Tatyana Fyodorova, deputy manager of Moscow's underground railway, helped, as a young woman, to build the railway with her own hands!

Consumer goods

A thing which appears strange to foreigners is that the people of so powerful a nation live so poorly. Things have improved enormously, but living standards in the Soviet Union are far below those of Russia's small neighbour, Finland.

To achieve its great success, the Soviet people had to make great sacrifices. While its important industries were being built, the people had to go without everyday articles, because the newly created factories concentrated on heavy industry. In carrying out the Five-Year Plans, as Soviet leaders have agreed, mistakes were made. And there were endless muddles about delivery. The Government has now learned many lessons, and the ordinary citizen, having got a refrigerator and television set, and paid a deposit on a car, is likely to demand more.

КОММУНИЗМ Я ЭТО СОВВЛАСТЬ 1974

Fuels for industry

◄ The Soviet Union is extremely rich in fuel materials. The main problem has been their uneven distribution.

Great changes have taken place since the days when the great reserves of wood and coal were the main sources of fuel. In recent years there have been great developments of oil production and natural gas. There has also been development of electrification, making use of cheap coal and oil. In recent years, the huge rivers have been harnessed to create electricity. The great hydro-electric power plant at Bratsk in Siberia was an important show-place, but it has now been overtaken by the even bigger station at Krasnoyarsk. Since its twelfth generator became operative in 1970 it produces 6 million kW!

▼ The production line of a Soviet car plant. Recently, FIAT was allowed to open a factory, but production in Russia still falls below Western levels. In such factories, as elsewhere women take an important share of the heavy work. These women are preparing to attach tail lights on the assembly line.

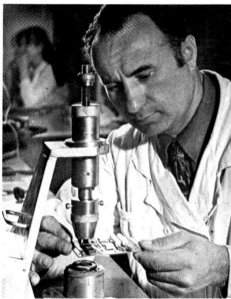

The treeless open area of the Russian and Ukrainian Steppes are ideal for the use of the most mechanized methods of cultivation. The top-soil is rich and produces wonderful crops. The Government has taken advantage of the position by abolishing private farms and establishing State farms and Collective farms. Even so, the country is sometimes short of grain. In an attempt to solve this problem, areas formerly thought too cold for grain, have been planted with specially hardy strains of wheat.

◄ An engineer with a drill, making parts for precision instruments. Heavy industry is the major area of production, though light industry and precision work have been growing. The fine parts for computers and aeronautic engineering require high levels of skill and long training.

▲ Transplanting felled conifers by tractor and trailer in Siberia. The Siberian forests produce great quantities of timber for use in wood-working and paper-making. Russia's great rivers, upon which the logs can be floated, help to solve the problem of transport over thousands of miles.

Some traditional crafts

Ashkabad carpet

Moldavian costume doll

Moldavian embroidery

Moldavian jug

Ukrainian bowl

Russian doll

▲ Traditional craftwork of the Soviet Union is familiar to visitors to the country. These include embroidery, carpets, decorated earthenware and the celebrated *matryoshka* dolls which can be opened to reveal several yet smaller dolls inside.

Character of the people

The Russians

The different nationalities of the Soviet Union have often different temperaments and different values as well. Russians, the largest group by far, often get on well with English people, and these two peoples are sometimes likened with each other. There is perhaps a similar sense of humour, a common interest in sport, a deeply-felt wish to avoid social friction, and a belief that good manners matter. People of both nations are practical and idealistic by turns. Russians, however, show their emotions more openly and may have rapid changes of mood from gleeful optimism and high spirits to the depths of despair. Russians have another quality unusual in any developed nation: that is a freedom from cynicism about human nature.

The crowded summer beaches on the Black Sea offer one clue to the Russian character. In Old Russia any village child was free to wander at will, and knew that he or she would find a welcome and food in any house. Russians have grown up feeling that they belong to a community. The modern Russian too is happiest in a group. And so, although people often have little choice, they endure cramped conditions with surprising tolerance. Russians who visit the West are often astonished by what they see.

Visitors are often repelled to be met by officials who do not smile, and by an attitude of sullen indifference. A Russian, if asked, will say, "Why should we smile if there is nothing to smile about? With you smiling is just a convention." But it is an attitude which can be broken, and one finds them to be *tot zhe sámy chútky, míly, otzývchivy naród*—the very same considerate, kind, sympathetic people—that the Russians were always reputed to be.

How the people see themselves

▲ Soviet people welcome an excuse for a party. It is likely to become very noisy and hilarious as the evening progresses and glasses are filled and refilled.

▲ People have lived with shortages for a long time, although things are better now. One might well have wanted to buy shoes to find only a big supply of shirts.

▼ Russians can be very impatient of trifles, yet tolerate great hardships with seeming indifference.

▼ Mother and grandmother play an important part in family life. Many families would find it impossible to manage without grandmother.

▲ Citizens regard themselves as protectors of the State. Sometimes they go too far, as here where the film is snatched from a tourist's camera.

50

▲ Children everywhere like to collect badges. These are Soviet examples. Some, like the Red Star of the young "Oktoberist" (in the centre) pledge the wearer to be kind and obedient. Others have to be earned by hard work.

▼ A rally of the local Communist Party in a public park. In addition to speeches on some political subjects, there will be songs and perhaps other entertainment.

▲ Children have a privileged place in Soviet Society, This statue, though a poor work of art, is intended to honour the citizens of tomorrow.

▲ People in the Soviet Union have a great respect for culture of all kinds. Music, particularly folk music, is popular, and many people play an instrument.

▲ The work of the Communist Party provides many opportunities for processions and flag-waving, and Party members pride themselves on their position.

New directions

▼ A wedding group. Weddings are always civil, not religious ceremonies, and couples wait their turn in the queue. As life becomes easier, people want more interesting ceremony in their lives. Many feel that weddings in Russia have been too austere in the past and want them made gayer and more attractive occasions.

▼ The Soviet Union is solving its housing problem by building many tall blocks of flats in the cities. Prefabricated parts speed the work. However, even the best-housed have only small flats. The cost of rent, gas and electricity, is low. It is possible to buy a house (but not the land it stands on) and the Government may help with a mortgage.

ВЕРТЯЩИЙСЯ СТУЛ ДЛЯ РАЗГОВОРА...

с вышестоящими

и нижестоящими.

ЗАЯВКА

Рисунок В. ТИЛЬМАНА

▲ Soviet socialist philosophy places great importance to the equality of individuals. However, officials may be high-handed with work-people, and subservient to party chiefs. Snobbery is a common human failing, which the magazine *Krokodil* here takes to task.

How the Soviet Union is changing

Many of the people who will take important jobs in the Soviet Union in the next few years have been born since the Revolution. They have lived under no other system, and they believe that the socialism they have inherited offers the best hope for a happy society. Therefore, Communism—however it may be modified—is likely to survive.

It is difficult for experts to forecast which way the Soviet Union will develop because the Government does not always announce its future plans.

The first impression is that the Soviet Union is content now to move forward to practical and realistic goals. Attempts—like the foolish one of Khrushchev to bring 70 million new acres under cultivation in two years—are not likely to be repeated. This suits the ordinary citizen, who, if asked, is likely to say that first of all he or she wants peace, and secondly, more and better goods in the shops.

The ordinary citizen

For the ordinary citizen life is very much freer. There are now not many topics he or she would need to be careful of talking about in public. People have more money to spend and more things to buy with it. To some extent, they have escaped the worst effects of world inflation. This is partly because the Soviet Union is to some extent independent of the rise of world prices; but goods on the free market, which people often prefer, are often three or four times the official price. And, even where prices are controlled, new models (at higher prices) are introduced, or consumers may find that the lower-priced grades are not available.

The Government is well aware that many of its brightest young people—even members of the Young Communist League—know a great deal about life in capitalist countries. The Government has tried to lead rather than instruct. It has given them a chance to air their views in the Komsomol newspaper, although foreigners might not think the paper entirely fair. When a reader wrote asking "Why is the Government spending millions on space research when I can't buy a decent pair of shoes?" it provided only space for readers who wanted to condemn this attitude. Perhaps the argument might develop into a discussion about how some of the real consumer problems might be solved without creating new troubles of the kind people in the West know so well.

▲ An oil storage plant in Siberia. Since the end of World War II, great strides have been made in developing this region. In spite of the extreme cold during the long winters, new towns and factories have been built to utilize Siberia's natural resources.

▶ Mr. Leonid Breznev, the Soviet Prime Minister meets President Gerald Ford of the U.S.A. While the two Super-Powers continue to regard each other with suspicion and try to extend their influence, they realize that any conflict would lead to disaster for the whole world.

▼ A Russian radar space-tracking ship in the Black Sea. This observes the movements of orbiting spacecraft. Russia not only has the most modern weapons for offensive and defensive action, but maintains a world-wide survey by satellite and surface vessels upon developments in space.

▲ Solzhenitsyn, the Russian author, has written novels critical of Soviet life. In 1974 controls were tightened and he was exiled. Here, he is seen with a friend, the German writer, Heinrich Bohl.

Reference
Human and physical geography

The climate of the Soviet Union

The map shows the main climatic regions. But one region merges very gradually in to the next, and there is great unformity of climate over large areas of the country. The special feature of the climate is the wide range of temperature between the intense cold of winter and the heat of summer; this is the continental type of climate which much of the Soviet Union experiences in an extreme form.

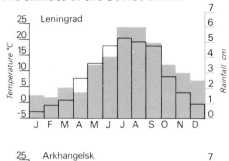

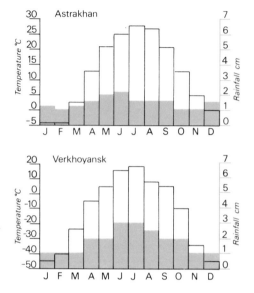

Climatic regions

The natural vegetation of the Soviet Union

Forest Vegetation
- Mixed Broad-leaved & Coniferous Forest
- Mixed Deciduous Forest
- Sub-tropical
- Wooded Steppe

Grass Vegetation
- Steppe
- Mountain Grassland

Desert Vegetation
- Semi-desert
- Desert
- Tundra

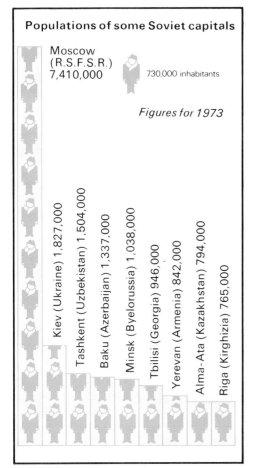

Populations of some Soviet capitals

Moscow
(R.S.F.S.R.)
7,410,000

730,000 inhabitants

Figures for 1973

Kiev (Ukraine) 1,827,000
Tashkent (Uzbekistan) 1,504,000
Baku (Azerbaijan) 1,337,000
Minsk (Byelorussia) 1,038,000
Tbilisi (Georgia) 946,000
Yerevan (Armenia) 842,000
Alma-Ata (Kazakhstan) 794,000
Riga (Kirghizia) 765,000

In 1973, the population of the Soviet Union was estimated to be 249 millions, of whom 146 million were town-dwellers, and 103 million lived in rural areas.

The population of the Soviet Union ranks third after that of China (730 million) and India (547 million). The Slavonic races make up three-quarters of the total population of the Soviet Union, and the Russians themselves number more than half. There are now sizeable Russian groups in nearly all the Republics of the Union, and they are in a position to influence the policies of these Republics, which remain theoretically independent.

The Revolution and two world wars have had their effect upon the population. In 1913 only 18 per cent of the people lived in towns. In 1970 the proportion had risen to 56 per cent. In recent years there has been an important movement of population to the new agricultural areas of Kazakhastan, and to the newly exploited areas, rich in mineral, water and timber resources, of Siberia.

◄ The capitals of the fifteen Soviet republics include the biggest city in the state — Moscow. However, some other major towns like Leningrad (4,313,000), Gorky (1,238,000) and Novosibirsk (1,221,000) are not capitals.

Densities of population

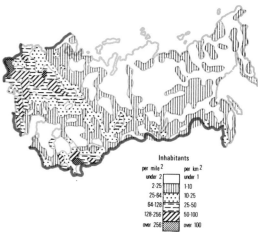

Inhabitants

per mile^2	per km^2
under 2	under 1
2-25	1-10
25-64	10-25
64-128	25-50
128-256	50-100
over 256	over 100

▲ Some areas of the Soviet Union are almost entirely without population. This includes much central and northern Siberia as well as the inhospitable regions of the Arctic. The high mountain areas of the Caucasus, in the south, which are impossible to cultivate, are thinly populated, and so too are some desert regions. The European part of the Soviet Union, west of the Urals, is by far the most densely populated. Six out of ten of all the people in the Soviet Union live in an area which is only one-sixth of the whole country.

Government

The Supreme Soviet is the highest law-making body in the Soviet Union. It consists of two Assemblies — the Soviet of the Union and the Soviet of Nationalities.

The Soviet of the Union is elected directly, with one deputy for every 300,000 electors. The Soviet of Nationalities is also elected by the citizens voting through their Union Republics or regional governments. The number of deputies alloted to each group depends upon its size. The highest executive and administrative body is the Council of Ministers which is appointed by the Supreme Soviet.

There is only one political party in the Soviet Union. This is the Communist Party. Not every Russian is a member of the Communist Party. It has only 14.8 million members, and 31 million belong to the Young Communist League.

At elections the Communist Party and other organisations can put forward names of candidates. After discussion this is usually reduced to one name. Electors are free to approve, or disapprove, of the choice in a secret ballot. In the 1970 election, 1,096 Communists and 421 non-party deputies were returned to the Supreme Soviet.

All effective control of the Government is in the hands of the Communist Party.

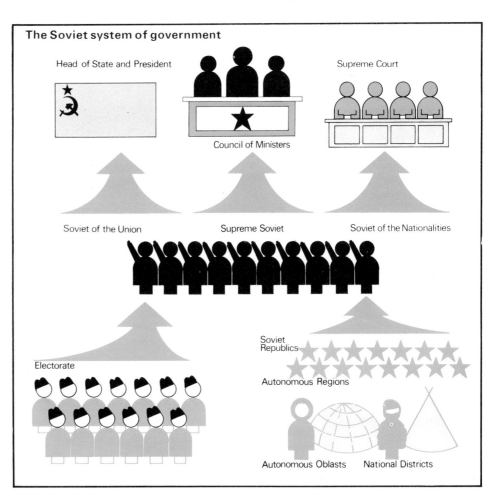

The Soviet system of government

Head of State and President

Council of Ministers

Supreme Court

Soviet of the Union

Supreme Soviet

Soviet of the Nationalities

Electorate

Soviet Republics

Autonomous Regions

Autonomous Oblasts

National Districts

Reference

History

THE RISE AND FALL OF THE RUSSIAN EMPIRE
A.D.

862	Norseman, Rurik, becomes Prince of Novgorod
882	State of Kiev Rus founded by Norseman, Oleg
988	Kiev Rus adopts Christianity
1147	First written mention of Moscow
1230	Kiev sacked by Monguls
1237-42	Mongul conquest of Russia
1240	Alexander Nevsky, Prince of Novgorod, defeated the Swedes on River Neva
1242	Mongol capital established on River Volga
1439	Russian Orthodox Church refuses union of Eastern and Western Churches
1462-1505	Ivan III, the Great, first Czar of Russia
1480	Mongols finally defeated.
1547	Ivan IV, the Terrible, crowned Czar of all the Russians
1552	Kazan (Mongol capital) destroyed; St. Basil's Cathedral, Moscow, built to commemorate victory
1581	Peasants lost right to change employers
1597	Serfdom established
1598-1605	Czar Boris Godunov reigns
1613	Michael Romanov elected Czar: the first of the great Romanov line
1657	Moscow regains control of Smolensk, Kiev and Ukraine
1670-71	Peasant revolt under the leadership of Stenka Rayin
1682-1725	Peter the Great rules
1703	St. Petersburg (afterwards Leningrad) founded by Peter the Great
1712	St. Petersburg becomes seat of government
1718-22	All land labourers become serfs. Poll tax on serfs introduced
1721	Treaty of Nystad—Russia makes peace and acquires Swedish lands
1722	Russia acquires western and southern shores of Caspian Sea
1755	Moscow University founded
1762-96	Reign of Catherine the Great
1773-4	Peasant revolt under Pugachov
1783	Crimea incorporated into Russia
1812	France invades Russia, Napoleon reaches Moscow.

	The great Winter Retreat by the French army
1825	Uprising by group of officers, "the Decembrists", aimed at political reform
1848	Karl Marx publishes the *Communist Manifesto*
1853-6	Crimean War
1861	Alexander II, the Liberator, abolishes serfdom
1867	Alaska sold by Russia to the United States
1870	Birth of Lenin
1887	Lenin's brother executed for plotting to assassinate Czar Alexander III
1891	Trans-Siberian Railway begun
1898	Social-Democratic (Marxist) Party formed
1900	Russia occupies Manchuria
1901	Widespread strikes in many of the principal cities
1903	Lenin forms Bolshevik group, by separating from the Mensheviks in the Social Democratic Party
1904-5	Russo-Japanese War which ends with Russian defeats on land and at sea
1905	A year of mass strikes, demonstrations. Mutiny aboard the battleship *Potemkin*
Jan.	St. Petersburg Revolt "Bloody Sunday"
Aug.	Czar promises the establishment of a *Duma* (Parliament)
Oct.	Czar issues Manifesto proclaiming decree of civil liberty. The Great General Strike
1906	First meeting of the Duma in the Czar's Winter Palace
1906-11	Introduction of land reforms
1912	Proposals for primary education for all
1914	Germany declares war on Russia.

THE BIRTH OF THE SOVIET UNION
1917

March 10	The "February"* Revolution. Troops riot in Petrograd (St. Petersburg until 1914). (*Using the old Julian Calendar. The new-style Georgian calendar, which is 10 days further on was not adopted until 1918. The Georgian Calendar has been used in the chronology.)
March 12-14	Provisional Government organised under Prince Lvov
March 15	Czar abdicates in favour of his brother Grand Duke Michael who in turn quickly abdicates in favour of Provisional Government
April 16	Lenin and other Bolshevik leaders arrive in Petrograd

July 11-18	Bolsheviks unsuccessful in attempt to seize power. Lenin goes into hiding in Finland. Trotsky is arrested
July 20	Prince Lvov resigns and Alexander Kerensky becomes Head of Provisional Government
Nov 6	The Bolshevik Revolution, the "October" Revolution. The Provisional Government headed by Kerensky overthrown and its members arrested. Lenin, Trotsky and Stalin head new regime known as the Council of People's Commissars
Dec. 6	Don Cossacks rebel. This rebellion marks the beginning of the Civil War which lasted until 1920. U.S.A., Britain, France and Japan supported the White Army against the Bolsheviks
1918	
March	Treaty of Brest-Litovsk with Central Powers. This ends the war for Russia, but deprives her of valuable resources and much territory
March	Moscow becomes capital of Russia again
July	Czar and his Family murdered
1919	Foundation of the Communist International (Comintern) to bring about world revolution
1921	Lenin announces the New Economic Policy (NEP) Suppression of Kronstadt Mutiny of the Baltic Fleet
1922	
April	Stalin becomes General Secretary of the Central Committee of the Communist party
Dec.	Soviet Union formed as a federation of the Soviet Republics
1924	Death of Lenin. Petrograd becomes Leningrad. Britain recognises Soviet Union

THE SOVIET UNION AFTER LENIN

1927	Trotsky expelled from the Communist Party
1928-32	First five-year plan; agriculture collectivized
1929	Trotsky exiled
1933-7	Second five-year plan
1933	U.S.A. recognizes Soviet Union
1934	U.S.S.R. becomes a member of the League of Nations
1935-8	Years of terror and purges
1936	New Constitution introduced
1939	Soviet-German non-aggression pact. U.S.S.R. invades Eastern Poland
1939-40	Soviet-Finnish war; Finland cedes territory to U.S.S.R.
1940	Estonia, Latvia, Lithuania

	incorporated into Soviet Union.
	Trotsky assassinated in Mexico City
1941	Soviet Union invaded by Germany
1942-3	Battle of Stalingrad; the Germans suffer major defeats
1949	U.S.S.R. explodes an atomic bomb. United Nations established with Soviet Union as member
1950	U.S.S.R. and China sign treaty of alliance
1953	Death of Stalin, and Stalin succeeded by Malenkov as Premier and First Secretary of the Party. Shortly afterwards, Khrushchev becomes First Secretary. U.S.S.R. explodes a hydrogen bomb
1954	U.S.S.R. negotiates agreement making important economic and political concessions to China
1955	Malenkov resigns as Premier and is replaced by Bulganin
1955	Warsaw Treaty establishes an equivalent to NATO among Eastern European and Soviet bloc
1956	Khrushchev attacks Stalin at the Twentieth Party Congress. Substantial break with Stalinist policies
1956	Soviet troops invade Hungary and put an end to the Hungarian uprising
1957	Soviet Union launches first space satellite
1958	Khrushchev takes over from Bulganin, becomes both Premier and First Secretary of the Party
1960	Sino-Soviet split
1961	Yuri Gagarin makes first manned space flight
1962	The Cuba crisis. Soviet missiles installed in Cuba
1963	U.S.S.R. and U.S.A. set up an emergency communication line between Moscow and Washington
1964	Khrushchev succeeded as First Secretary by Brezhnev and as Premier by Kosygin
1965	A Soviet astronaut makes the first space walk
1967	Fiftieth anniversary of the Bolshevik revolution
1968	Spring revolution in Czechoslovakia. Soviet tanks invade Prague
1969	Soviet and Chinese troops clash in border disputes
1974	Soviet Union buys huge quantities of wheat from Canada
	Solzenitsyn exiled
1975	Trade treaty with Britain. Bulganin dies

The Arts

LITERATURE

Lomonosov, Mikhail (1711-65) poet, chemist and mathematician. Founder of modern literary Russian by establishing a literary Russian language, which combined the Slavonic usage of the church with spoken Russian. *Ode on the Taking of Khotin from the Turks.*

Krylov, Ivan (1769-1844) fables. First Russian author to sell works in tens of thousands.

Pushkin, Alexander (1799-1837) poet. *Evgeny Onegin; The Bronze Horseman, The Captain's Daughter.*

Gogol, Nikolai (1809-1852) novelist. *Dead Souls; The Inspector-General.*

Lermontov, Mikhail (1814-41) dramatist, poet, novelist. *A Hero of Our Times.*

Turgenev, Ivan (1818-83) novelist. *Fathers and Sons, On the Eve, Smoke.*

Goncharov, Ivan (1812-91) novelist. *Oblomov.*

Dostoevsky, Fedor (1821-81) novelist. *Crime and Punishment; The Possessed; The Idiot; The Brothers Karamazov.*

Tolstoi, Lev (1828-1910) novelist, fablist. *War and Peace; Anna Karenina; Resurrection.*

Chekhov, Anton (1860-1904) playwright, short-story writer. *Uncle Vanya; The Cherry Orchard; Three Sisters.*

Blok, Alexander (1880-1921) greatest of the Russian Symbolist poets.

Mandelstam, Osip (1891-1940?) among the greatest of 20th century Russian poets. Leading member of Acmeist school of poets.

Akhmatova, Anna (1888-1966) poet. Another of leaders of Acmeist school. *Poem without a hero.*

Gorky, Maxim (1868-1936) novelist, short-story writer. Autobiography *Childhood, My Apprenticeship, My Universities.*

Essenin, Sergei (1895-1925) poet.

Mayakovsky, Vladimir (1893-1930) poet; put much of talents at disposal of Revolution. Satirized contemporary Russia in two plays *The Bath House,* and *The Bed Bug.*

Pasternak, Boris (1890-1960) novelist, poet. *Dr. Zhivago.* Refused to be drawn into contemporary politics. Nobel prize-winner.

Ostrovski, N. A. (1904-36) novelist. *How the Steel was Tempered.*

Sholokhov, M. A. (1905-) reputed author of *And Quiet Flows the Don.*

Solzenitsyn, Alexander (1918-) author. *First Circle; Cancer Ward; Day in the Life of Ivan Denisovich; August 1914.* Nobel prize-winner.

Yevtuskenko, Evgeny (1933-) poet. *Babi Yar; Stalin's Heirs.*

MUSIC

Glinka, Mikhail (1804-57) composer of operas. *A Life for the Czar; Ruslan and Ludmilla, Prince Kholmsky.*

Borodin, Alexander (1839-87) composed opera, *Prince Igor* and chamber music.

Mussorgsky, Modest (1839-81) composer of *Boris Godunov, Pictures from an Exhibition.*

Tchkaikowsky, Peter (1840-93) composer of symphonies, ballet scores etc. *Swan Lake, Nutcracker Suite.*

Rimsky-Korsakov, Nicholas (1844-1908) writer of folk-songs, operas, symphonic poems and church music. *Scheherezade.*

Rachmaninov, Sergei (1873-1943) symphonies, operas and songs, concertos and church music.

Stravinsky, Igor (1882-1971) composer of symphonies, ballet music. *Firebird, Rite of Spring, Lady Macbeth of Mtensk.*

Khachaturian, A. (1903-) popular exponent of Armenian music.

Prokofiev, Sergei (1891-1953) symphonies, concertos, ballet music. *Peter and the Wolf; Love of Three Oranges.*

Shostakovitch, Dimitri (1906-) composer of symphonies.

PAINTING, ARCHITECTURE, ETC

Vladimir Mother of God, 12th c. icon. The most venerated of Russian icons.

Cathedral of St. Dimitri, Vladimir, 1194-7.

Cathedral of the Dormitron, 1475-9. Central cathedral of the Kremlin, Moscow.

Church of the Transfiguration, Kizhi, 1714. A church with intricate designs built entirely of wood.

Voronikhin, A. (1760-1814) architect. Built Cathedral of Our Lady of Kazan, Leningrad.

Shubin, Fedot (1740-1805) sculptor.

Levitski, D. (1735-1822) fashionable portrait painter.

Repin, I. (1884-1930) painter. *The Volga Boatmen; The Religious Procession.*

Surikov, V. (1848-1916) painter. *Boyarina Morozova.*

Benois, Alexandre (1870-1960) painter. *Fantasy on a Versailles theme.*

Serov, V. (1864-1911) painter. *Portrait of a girl with peaches.*

Kandinsky, V. (1866-1944) abstract expressionist painter. Went into exile in 1922.

Malevich, K. (1878-1935) abstract artist. *Woman with a rake; The Scissors Grinder; Dynamic Suprematism.*

Tatlin, V. (1885-1953) proceeded from painting, via applied art to the design of clothing, pottery and furniture.

Larionov, M. (1881-1964) painter; leading figure in Rayonism school.

Popova, L. (1889-1924) leading Cubist painter in Russia. *The Traveller.*

Golosov, P. A. (1902-) architect. Designed *Pravda* building in style of Le Corbusier. When contemporary movements in art were forbidden by Soviet Government, Golosov fell into line and produced nothing further of importance.

Reference

The Economy

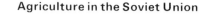

FACTS AND FIGURES

Main trading partners: over 60% with Comecon countries of Eastern Europe, particularly East Germany, Poland and Hungary.
Currency: No free exchange rate for the rouble. For foreign trade 1 rouble =$U.S. 1.33 or £0.56.
Budget: revenue (1972) 175,100 m. roubles. Expenditure 173,200 m. (defence 17,900 m.; social, and cultural services 62,900 m.; national expenditure 82,600 m.
National income: 152,900 m. roubles in 1961; 315,200 m. in 1972.
Comecon: (Council for Mutual Economic Assistance). The Soviet Union is a founder member. The organization includes Bulgaria, Czechoslovakia, Hungary, Poland, Rumania, Cuba, East Germany and Mongolia.

Legend:

Wheat	Potatoes	Cotton
Millet	Rice	Flax
Maize	Sugar Beet	Tobacco
Rye	Tea	

Principal Fishing Ports	
Cattle	
Pigs	
Sheep	

Soviet trade

From the outset, the Soviet Government aimed at being economically self-sufficient, and until the 1950s foreign trade was minimal. This was possible because the country could produce most essentials, and because the Government controlled trade and the means of production.

Recently, foreign trade has grown as the Soviet Union was able to exploit new resources. This has helped to increase the speed of development, and to improve the standard of living. Even so, foreign trade in 1973 (exports 15,800 million; imports 15,500 m.) was only about a quarter of the total of that of the United States.

Trade with countries in the Soviet bloc accounted for more than half of the Soviet Union's imports in 1973. Bulky articles, like fuels, timber, ores, concentrates and metals make up about 40% of exports. Flour and grain have declined as export articles since the Revolution, and recently the Soviet Union has imported grain. Machinery, planes and other equipment make up about 20% of exports.

Machinery and industrial and transport equipment, coming mainly from industrialized Eastern European countries, account for about 40% of imports, and foodstuffs and consumer goods make up another 30%.

Imports and exports

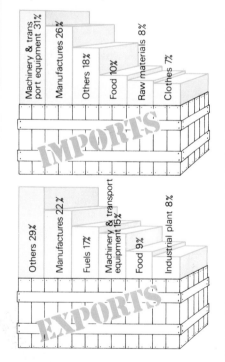

Imports: Machinery & transport equipment 31%, Manufactures 26%, Others 18%, Food 10%, Raw materials 8%, Clothes 7%

Exports: Others 29%, Manufactures 22%, Fuels 17%, Machinery & transport equipment 15%, Food 9%, Industrial plant 8%

Imports: The Soviet Union consistently imports more than it exports. Oil imports are increasing rapidly, and becoming more expensive.

▲ **Agriculture.** Nearly all the agricultural land in the Soviet Union belongs to the State. Huge farms have now taken the place of the old peasant farms, and the peasants who have chosen to live in village communities, are housed by the State. They are now also paid by the State. The farms are of two kinds: Collective farms and State farms. On the Collectives, the farmers lease the land from the state, and elect a committee to manage the farm. Equipment, livestock and buildings belong to the Collective. Nowadays, workers receive a guaranteed monthly sum: before they only earned what was left after the State had taken its quota of their produce.

The State farms are owned and operated by the State. They are generally bigger, and are set up to develop new land, or engage in research to improve agriculture. In recent years there has been a tendency for Collectives to amalgamate and become State farms. The State farms are better equipped with farm machinery.

On the Collectives, every farmer has a small plot for his own use. These plots provide the towns with produce, and there are constant complaints that farmers neglect their communal work for their plots.

Wheat, barley and rye are widely grown, although fodder crops have recently been encouraged to help animal rearing. Potatoes are grown in colder areas.

► **Industry.** At the time of the Revolution, Russia was making some progress towards becoming an industrial country, but its industry was limited in range and distribution. The Soviet Government then set itself the task of making the country an industrial giant. At first much of the industry was almost exclusively concentrated in the old towns of the west, principally in European Russia and the Ukraine.

The Germans invaded in 1941, and many of the most valuable industries were destroyed by the invaders, or by the Soviet people themselves, trying to prevent the Germans from capturing their equipment. So, after 1942, important new centres of industry were built beyond the Urals, out of reach of invaders from Europe. This trend has continued because the development of special industrial regions saves costs.

Until recently most of the Soviet effort was directed towards heavy industry. Now more emphasis is placed on consumer goods and other things that make life more comfortable. Even so, production runs too far behind demand to satisfy most people.

Some economists have suggested that production would increase if competition between factories were allowed. Naturally, in the Soviet Union, this view has many critics: because competition creates its own kind of waste, and because Soviet philosophy encourages industries to work in partnership, not competition.

Industry in the Soviet Union

Symbol	Legend
	Major Industrial Centres
	Mechanical Engineering
	Automobiles
	Shipbuilding
	Locomotives
	Precision Instruments
	Cement
	Paper
	Aeroplanes
	Electrical Machinery
	Textiles
	Principal Coalmining Areas
	Iron Metallurgy
	Chemicals
	Natural Gas
	Oil Refineries
	Nuclear Power

How people are employed

Total population 246m

Non working population 136m

Coal mining 1m
Iron steel 1.1m
Chemicals 1.2m
Building materials 1.7m
Textiles 4.2m
Food processing 2.4m
Machinery & metal work 9m
Agriculture 28m
Services, armed forces, other industries 61m

Employed population 110m
Over 50% are women

◄ **Employment.** Three things which stand out about the labour position in the Soviet Union are: firstly, the high proportion of women employed, often in heavy, manual work, and sometimes in very responsible positions. They form more than half of the work force, and in some professions far outnumber men. Secondly, about a quarter of all workers are engaged in agriculture, compared with about 5% in the United States and about 2% in Britain. Thirdly, defence makes heavy demands both in manpower and resources.

The total number of people employed is about 110 million. This is more than a third more than in the United States, but output per worker in the Soviet Union is lower. This is partly because Soviet industry is less highly mechanised, and partly because the hard Russian winter limits out-of-door work for part of the year. Also, in the Soviet Union there is very little unemployment. To avoid unemployment, the State goes to great lengths to find jobs for everyone, even when this means putting people into situations where they have very little to do.

In the Soviet Union trade unions do not make wage claims. Wages are calculated on the value of the industry to the economy as a whole; partly on its location, with higher rates for remote, harsh areas; partly on the unpleasantness of conditions in which some people have to work; and partly on the individual's skill and qualifications.

Gazetteer

Alma-Ata (4 20N 76 50E) Cap. of the Kazakh S.S.R. on the Turksib Railway. Pop. (1973) 794,000. Trade in wheat, sugar-beet, apples, grapes. Manufactures machinery, textiles. City built as a fort by Russians in 1854. Damaged in earthquakes, 1887 and 1911.

Archangelsk (64 35N 40 50E) Pop. (1973) 362,000. Founded 1553. Russia's only seaport until 1703. Railway built in 1897. Port frozen December-April, kept open in May and Nov. by ice-breakers. Leading supply port in both World Wars.

Azov Sea (45 53N 35 35E) Ancient Palus (Swamp) Maeotis. Connected to Black Sea by the Strait of Kerch. Frozen around shores Nov.-March. Important fisheries.

Baikal, Lake (53 0N 108 0E) Largest freshwater lake in Asia: deepest lake in the world. Greatest depth 1,600 m. (5,300 ft.). Frozen 4 months a year: otherwise navigable to steamers. Sturgeon, herring, salmon. Contains forms of life to be found nowhere else.

Baku (40 27N 49 48E) Cap, of Azerbaijanian S.S.R., on the Caspian Sea. Pop. (1973) 1,337,000. Important sea-port and oil-producing centre. Shipbuilding, oil-drilling equipment, chemicals, cement, textiles. Oil pipes to Batumi. Ships oil to Astrakhan. Founded before 10th Century. University 1919. Academy of Sciences 1945. Russian since 1806.

Caspian Sea (42 30N 51 0E) World's largest inland sea. North, east, west coasts are in U.S.S.R. No outlet. Tideless. Frozen 2-3 months a year in north. Salt deposits on Kara Bogaz Gol, in east. Famous for caviare.

Dnieper, River (47 0N 33 35E) 3rd longest in Europe: 2,250 km. (1,400 miles). Navigable as far as Dorogobuzh. Frozen 3-4 months a year.

Don, River (50 0N 42 0E) Ancient R. Tanals. 1,900 km. (1,200 miles) long. Linked by canal to R. Volga. Ice 3-4 months a year. Fisheries. Transport of grain, coal, timber.

Dushanbe (38 20N 68 30E) Cap. of Tadzhik S.S.R. Pop. (1973) 411,000. Meat-packing. Manufactures textiles, machinery, cement, leather.

Frunze (42 55N 75 0E) Cap. of Kirghiz S.S.R., on a branch of the Turksib Railway. Pop. (1973) 463,000. Manufactures agricultural machinery, textiles. Founded in 19th century as Pishpek and renamed after Revolutionary leader.

Gorky (56 17N 44 0E) Birthplace of Maxim Gorky. Pop (1973) 1,238,000. River-port and railway junction. Manufactures cars, locomotives, aircraft. Oil-refining. Ship-building. Founded 1221 as Nizhni Novgorod.

Kharkov (49 50N 36 15E) Pop. (1973) 1,307,000. Manufactures tractors, agricultural machinery. Coal-mining, oil-drilling. Founded 17th century. Severely damaged in 2nd World War.

Kiev (50 24N 30 28E) Cap of Ukrainian S.S.R. and 3rd largest city of U.S.S.R. Pop. (1973) 1,827,000. Port on Dnieper. Rail and road junction. Founded before 9th century. 11th century cathedral and monastery. University 1833. Manufactures machinery, chemicals, textiles, clothing.

Kishinev (47 2N 28 52E) Cap. of Moldavian S.S.R. Pop (1973) 415,000. Food-processing. Leather, footwear, hosiery. Founded 1436. Joined U.S.S.R. in 1940.

Kuibyshev (53 12N 50 0E) Pop. (1973) 1,117,000. River-port, airport, railway junction. Oil-refining, flour-milling. Aircraft, tractors, chemicals, textiles. Hydroelectric power station. Government transferred here during Second World War. Founded as Samara: re-named in 1935 after V. V. Kuibyshev.

Ladoga, Lake (61 30N 31 0E) Largest lake in Europe: 201 km. (125 m.) long. Frozen Dec.-March. Canals to Volga and Baltic Sea. Fisheries.

Lena, River (64 30N 127 0E) U.S.S.R.'s longest river: 4,300 km. (2,650 m.) Navigable for 3,900 km. Delta ice-bound November-June.

Leningrad (60 0N 30 25E), at mouth of R. Neva. Pop. (1973) 4,313,000. Founded in 1703 as St. Petersburg. Capital until 1918. Renamed Petrograd 1914. Became Leningrad in 1924. U.S.S.R.'s 2nd largest city. Ice-bound Dec.-March. Ship-building, machinery, chemicals, textiles. Fur trade. Exports timber. University 1819. Hermitage Art Gallery, Winter Palace, Peter and Paul Fort. Under siege 1941-4.

Minsk (54 0N 27 30E) Cap. of Byelorussian S.S.R. Pop. (1973) 1,038,000. Railway junction. Manufactures cars, tractors, machinery, ball bearings, radio sets. Academy of Sciences 1929. Taken from Poland in 1793. Severe damage in 2nd World War.

Moscow (55 50N 37 40E) Capital of Russian F.S.S.R. and U.S.S.R. Pop. (1973) 7,410,000. Burned in 1812 in French invasion. Industrial expansion in 19th century. Manufactures textiles, cars, aircraft, machinery, chemicals, paper. Government offices. Many cathedrals, museums, theatres. State Opera House. Academy of Sciences. Underground railway opened in 1935.

Novosibirsk (55 10N 83 5E) Largest city in Siberia. Pop. (1973) 1,221,000 Manufactures agricultural and mining machinery, lorries, bicycles, textiles. Sawmilling, flour-milling, brewing. Trade in grain, meat, butter.

Okhotsk, Sea (57 0N 149 0E) Arm of N.W. Pacific on east coast of Siberia. Area 600,000 sq. m. North ice-bound November-May.

Onega, Lake (60 40N 37 30E) 2nd largest lake in Europe. Canals to Volga and White Sea. Frozen December-March. Fisheries.

Riga (56 58N 24 12E) Cap. of Latvian S.S.R. 2nd most important Baltic port. Pop. (1973) 765,000. Exports timber, flax, paper, butter, eggs. Manufactures footwear, cement, rubber goods, telephonic equipment, paper, textiles. Ship-building. Harbour closed by ice about 4 months a year. Bathing beaches.

Founded 12th century. Polish in 1561: Swedish in 1621: Russian in 1710. Occupied by German forces 1941-4.

Sverdlovsk (56 52N 60 32E) Pop. (1973) 1,099,000. Railway junction and chief cultural centre of Urals. Manufactures heavy engineering equipment, ball bearings, lathes, railway rolling stock, aircraft, chemicals, clothing, furniture. Copper smelting, gem-cutting and polishing. Founded in 1721 as Ekaterinburg. Re-named 1924.

Tashkent (41 7N 69 15E) Cap. of Uzbek S.S.R. Largest city in Soviet Central Asia. Pop. (1973) 1,504,000. Products—cotton, silk, rice. Manufactures textiles, agricultural machinery, leather goods, paper. Coal, hydro-electric plants. Ruins of Muslim seminaries. Taken by Russia in 1865.

Tbilisi (41 45N 44 48E) Cap. of Georgian S.S.R. Pop. (1973) 946,000. Engineering, woodwork, textiles, electrical equipment. At Zemo-Avchala power from hydro-electric station. Trade in carpets, dried fruit. Founded 5th century. Passed to Russia in 1800.

Ural Mountains (59 0N 60 0E) System extends over 2,250 km. (1,400 m.) N-S from Arctic Ocean. Part of physical boundary between Asia and Europe. Generally low elevation. Highest point is Narodnaya (1,900 metres). Forests; iron, manganese, nickel, copper deposits.

Verkhoyansk (68 0N 133 30E) Town on R. Yana. Furs, mining. Former place of exile Lowest winter temperature outside Antarctica. Has registered −37°C (−100°F).

Vilnius (54 42N 25 15E) Cap. of Lithunanian S.S.R. Pop. (1973) 409,000. Railway junction. Saw-milling, food-processing, agricultural implements, fertilizers, paper. University founded 1579. Cathedral, churches, synagogues, a mosque. Became Russian in 1795 following the partition of Poland.

Vladivostok (42 58N 131 50E) Pop. (1973) 481,000. Founded 1860. Chief seaport and naval base on Pacific Coast. Fishing, whaling, ship-building, sawmilling, fish-canning. Harbour kept open in winter by ice-breakers.

Volga, River (57 30N 42 0E) Longest river in Europe: 3,900 km. (2,425 m.), and most important in U.S.S.R. Navigable along almost entire length. Irrigation, hydroelectric power. Sturgeon and other fish. Closed by ice 3-5 months a year.

Yablonovy Range (52 0N 114 0E) In S.E. Siberia east of L. Baikal. Extends S.W.—N.E. about 113 km. (700 m.). Part of watershed for rivers flowing to the Arctic and Pacific. Average height 1,200-1,800 metres.

Yenisei, River (72 20N 80 0E) 3,900 km. (2,400 m.) long. Flows into the Arctic Ocean. Navigable along its whole length. Lower reaches ice-free only July-Oct. Transport of timber and grain.

Yerevan (40 10N 44 20E) Cap. of Armenian S.S.R. Pop. (1973) 842,000. Chemicals, machinery, tyres, textiles. Aluminium refining. Powered from plants on Zenga River; natural gas from Karadag. Russian since 1827. Many Turkish and Persian buildings.

Index

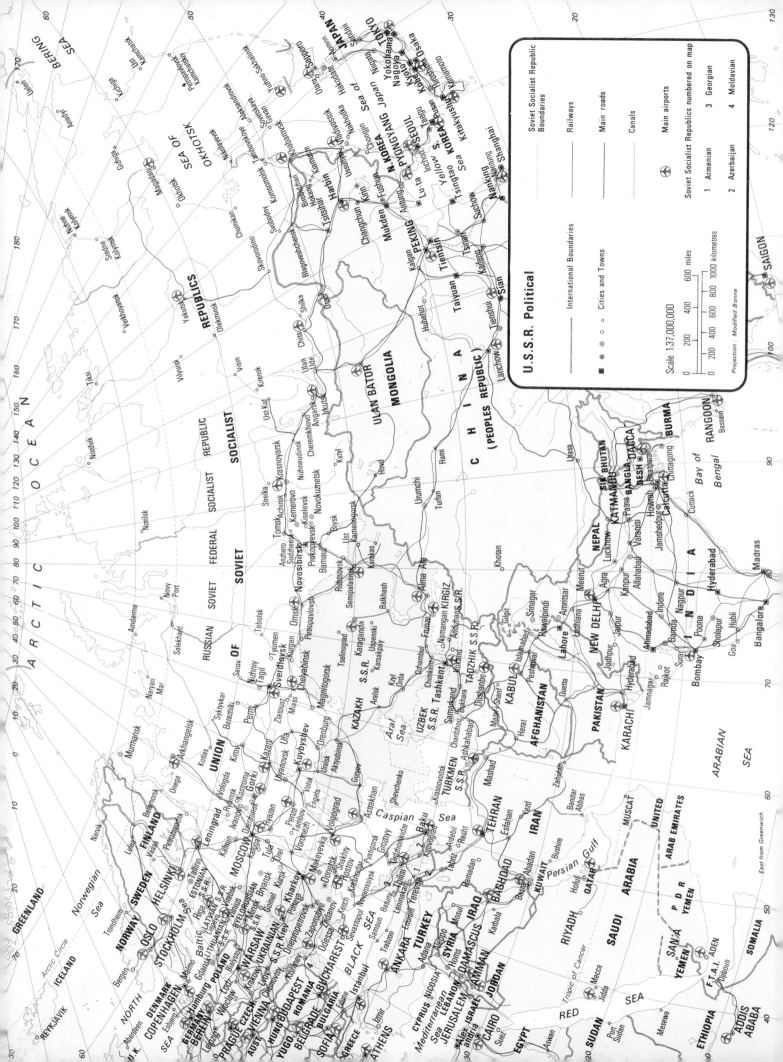

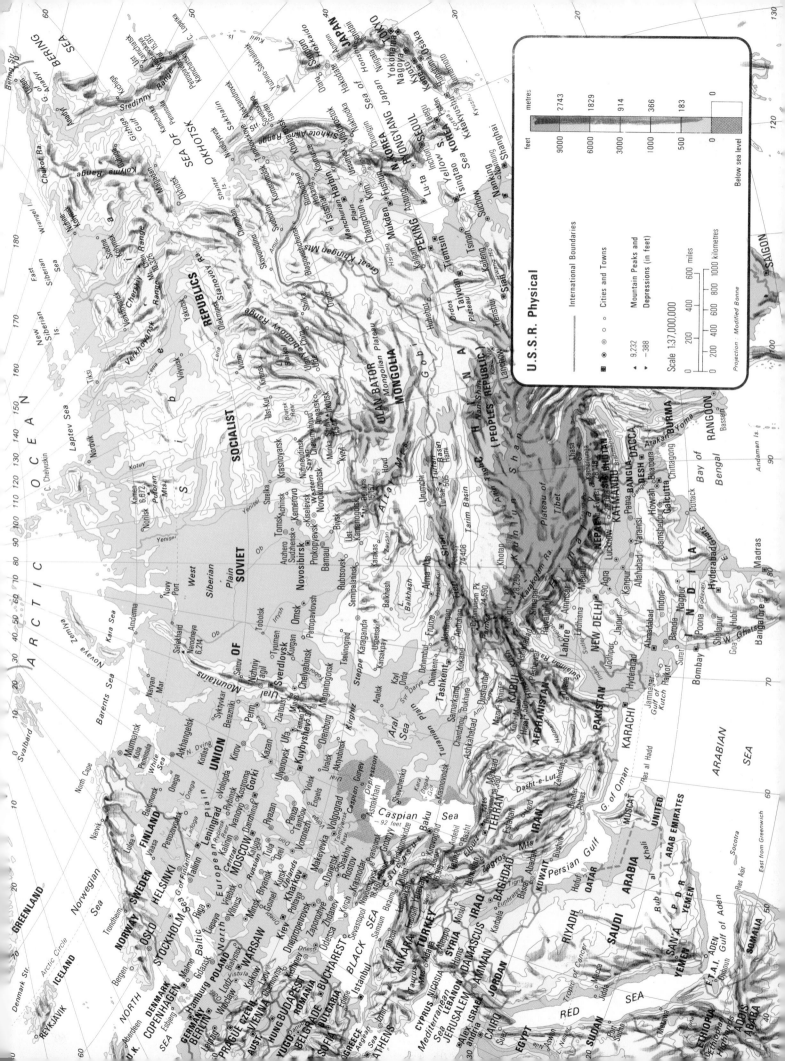

1 2 3 4 5 6 7 8 9 10-McN-81 80 79 78 77 76